Tell Me Why!

By Nessie Wallace

Nessie Wallace

Copyright

Nessie Wallace

Published 2015

Cover: Joshua Scott Brown – JSB Designs

Formatted: Brenda Wright, Formatting Done Wright

Tell Me Why! is a work of fiction. All names, characters, places and events portrayed in this book either are from the author's imagination or are used fictitiously. Any similarity to real persons, living or dead, establishments, events, or location is purely coincidental and not intended by the author. Please do not take offence to the content, as it is FICTION.

Trademarks: This book identifies product names and services known to be trademarks, registered trademarks, or service marks of their respective holders. The authors acknowledges the trademarked status in this work of fiction. The publication and use of these trademarks is not authorized, associated with, or sponsored by the trademark owners.

Table of Contents

Dedication

I would like to dedicate this book to the children in Foster care, and my four children I adopted in 2009. They were also in foster care. I can't tell you how they have changed my life.

Tell Me Why!

Nessie Wallace

Prologue

Tim and Liz

As we traveled back from Mississippi with my mother's ashes I began to remember the many trips I took in my younger years. I had fallen in love at first sight with the most beautiful woman in the world, but she lived in Texas and I lived in Mississippi. I married her as soon as I could. Well, as soon as I got her dad's blessing. Thinking about my mother no longer living makes me realize I only have two living family members, my wife Elizabeth, and our daughter, Jenna. Without them I would be all alone in this big old world. I don't know what I would do without them.

Jenna, was not feeling well so we had her stay at home. Now, her mother and I are worried about her so we decided not to stay the night so we can get home to check on her. It's late so engaging in conversation with Liz about our fondest memories will insure that I stay awake for our long trip home.

"I can't believe this is our last trip back from Mississippi. I never in a million years would have dreamed that I'd find the love of my life outside of my hometown." I turn and smile at my bride of twenty-five years. She's a Texas girl with Louisiana traits. Her mother was from Louisiana, and was one hell of a cook. She married a man from Texas. He loved her cooking so much he opened up a café. He wanted to share with everyone what he believed to be the best cooking in the world. That's where I met my Elizabeth. I laughed when he told me that story, but I am so happy she taught my Liz to cook.

"The trip from Mississippi to Texas seemed to get longer and longer every time I made it while courting you."

Liz smiles back "I was worth every traveled mile wasn't I?" I nodded. She was worth so much more. One look at her and she captivated my heart.

"My love you were worth more than anything in this world. You brought me to my knees the moment I saw you. I remember thinking, *she must be a model.* I didn't think I had a fighting chance of you giving me a second look."

"You were the most handsome man I had ever laid eyes on. I never dreamed you were interested in me until you came back every week for the next two months. My mother told me you had eyes for me. I thought you were way out of my league. Did you know I nearly passed out when you asked me out to dinner? When I got to the kitchen Mom asked me if

I had seen a ghost. She said I was whiter than Casper. But she understood when I told her you had asked me out."

I think I just blushed. This woman is the only person who could do this to me. "My palms were so sweaty, Liz. My mouth felt like I had just eaten a handful of sand. Rick had me practice asking you out. I think we practiced an hour before I got out of the car. Then I practiced all the way to the door." She giggles, and her giggle is music to my ears.

"Tim, baby, that invitation was nothing compared to your proposal. I do believe you were on your knees for ten minutes. You just kept opening and closing your mouth. I think I said yes before you said will you."

She's right. I was so afraid she would say no that the words refused to leave my throat. I was so in love then and that love has only grown deeper. The only other woman that has ever held my heart besides Liz is my amazing daughter, Jenna. She has me wrapped around her little finger and I am not ashamed to say it.

"You remember the first time we got to hold our little Jenna, and all the promises we made her that day?" Liz nods her head and smiles. "I think we have kept most of those promises. We said she could have anything she ever asked for, and we told her she could sleep with us until she was five. I was so happy she wanted to be a big girl at three and move into her own room. I clearly remember that day too! You knew I loved having our baby girl in our room, but the fun you and I had together once she starting sleeping in her own bed was and still is amazing."

Her face lights up with only the mention of Jenna's name. "How could I forget the happiest day of our lives? If I am not mistaken, that was the first time I ever saw you cry. I could tell she would be the apple of your eye." I chuckled at that. She was right. "I sure hope she finds an amazing husband and father for her children. I am not sure they make them like you anymore." I'm not sure if I want to smile or cry at that comment. I am not ready for my baby girl to have a steady boyfriend, much less a husband and a child.

"GOD, TIM! WATCH OUT..."

Chapter 1

Jenna

It was a rainy night in Houston, when the call came. My grandmother Mattie, from Mississippi had passed away. Grandma Mattie was my father's mother. She was the last living grandparent I had. Both Mom and Dad were the only children their parents had. Mom had one other pregnancy besides me, but had a miscarriage at three and a half months. So being an only child was something we all had in common.

Mom and Dad met while he was in the military. My mom said Dad was the most handsome man she had ever seen. Dad says Mom looked like a model that had just stepped off of the runway. He said she turned every head in the room.

It was by sheer accident that he had found her. He and three of his military brothers were passing through Houston on their way to Mississippi. They were just outside of Houston when the hummer they were in had a blow out. They changed the tire and Rick decided he was hungry. According to dad, Rick was always hungry. Dad tried to explain to him that they didn't have time to stop and eat because they were already running behind their scheduled time. Rick began to argue and pointed to a small mom and pop dinner across the road, arguing "we can get a bite there and be on our way." Dad eventually gave in and walked across the road.

Mom was in college but helped her parents at the diner when she had some free time, which wasn't often. Dad said that one look at her and he knew he was a goner. Mom said she smiled and thought to herself, "*My God, I must be dreaming,* He has to be lost!" She was so sure he would never give her a second look. He was a man that you could only dream about having. Needless to say, Dad took every mission that required him to go anywhere near Houston, until his military service was up. He and Mom were married two years later.

These memories are all I have to hold onto now. Mom and Dad had been on their way home from picking up Grandma Mattie's ashes, when a drunk driver crossed over the yellow line hitting them head on. They were both killed on impact.

I answered the door to find a Houston Police Officer asking if I was Jenna Kingsley. I nodded and he began to tell me about the accident. All I can remember was the officer saying, "I'm sorry Miss Kingsley, but your parents were both killed in an accident." He assured me they never felt a thing. Everything else was a blur. I grabbed my stomach and fell to my knees and cried "WHY? God, Why now? Why take them when I needed them most!"

Now I blankly stare out of the window, lost in my own world. My best friend since first grade, Angel, has agreed to drive me down to Galveston. This is where I will spread Mom and Dad's ashes, at our beach house where we spent many summers. Mom loved the beach. She always said when she watched the sun go down on the water that it had to be the closest place to Heaven she could get without dying. So what better place to spread their remains?

Angel has tried to start a conversation a few times since we left Houston, but talking is not for me right now.

"Jen, you really need to get out of that head of yours." I know she's right. All I have at this moment is my memories. It scares me to think that one day those will also be gone.

Angel tries to break the silence again with turning the radio on. After five words into the song I reach over and turn the radio off. The sound system in the two month old Camaro Mom and Dad gave me is bad ass, but right now all I want is to hear my parents voices. I want to hear my father say, *"Jenna Lynn, you come down here and help your mom in the* kitchen," or my mom say, *"It's all going to be okay Jen, just have a little faith."*

Tears begin streaming down my face, and I can do nothing to stop them. I cry silently for a while and turn to look at Angel. I decide at that moment that it is time to tell someone. "Angel, I'm pregnant," it just rolls off of my tongue. Angel's mouth falls open, but nothing comes out. I know I have just shocked my best friend for the first time in twelve years.

I watch as Angel closes and opens her mouth again, and wonder if a cat got her tongue. She slows down and pulls over to the side of the highway. As she puts the car in park, she throws her arms around my neck. I can feel her tears in my hair, and I know she feels my pain. Without any words, she tells me she loves me and will always be there when I need her.

Angel loosens her grip on my neck and wipes her tears. She looks at me, with a huge shaky smile that says, "It's going to be okay." Then the words start to flood my ears as she finds her voice. "Jen, I can't believe it! When? How? Who? Why didn't you tell me?" All I can do is hang my head in shame. I am not ashamed of my baby, but ashamed that I had broken the promise Angel and I made to each other. We had promised one another that we would talk to each other before we gave up our virginity. We had a pact to try to talk one another out of it. This would guarantee that we were ready, and that we were choosing the right person.

"I'm sorry Angel," is all that comes out before she hauls me into a bear hug. We both cry a little more and I know it's time to come clean with her and tell her the whole story. I will give her every detail, but at this moment I just need to feel her love and support. Angel would never judge me for what I've done, but the thought of letting down the three most important people in my life has my heart in shreds.

She whispers in my ear, "It's going to be okay, Jen. Let's just get to Galveston and we can talk about it there." I hold her tighter and nod my head. We used some napkins that she had grabbed when we stopped for breakfast to wipe away our tears.

When we are back on the road again, I feel her hand touch my little baby bump and I turn to see her smile. "I can't believe I'm going to be a nanny at seventeen!" I give her a sad smile and she chuckles, "He or she is going to love Nanny Angel because I will spoil them rotten." She can't control her little giggles as she removes her hand.

Continuing on, we are back to silence again and I wonder what Angel's thinking, but I don't ask. I just turn and stare out of the window like I had been for the past hour. I leave her alone with her thoughts to let it all sink in. I know this has to be hard on her; our friendship has always been based on honesty and trust.

As we pull into the driveway of the beach house, my heart does a flip and my tears begin to stream again. Opening my door, I will my body to get out of the car. I begin rethinking my choice of coming back here this soon. My heart knows this is the perfect spot to spread Mom and Dad's ashes. This beach is where Dad brought Mom on their honeymoon. It's also the place where I was conceived. I know Mom would be proud of me for this.

Angel comes around and grabs a hold of my hand, to let me know that I'm not alone. I give her hand a squeeze, silently saying, thank you. We take the stairs up slowly, knowing I won't be able to see their smiling faces. It pulls at something deep within my soul, but I keep going because I know in my heart I have to do this.

Once inside I walk straight to my room and lie across my bed and cry. Angel sits on the edge of the bed. She gently rubs my back and says, "Let it go, Jen. I can't even imagine the pain you have at this moment, and I wish I could take it all away. I know it's not possible, I just want you to know I am here if you need me."

I lay here for what seems like hours, which really has only been a few minutes. Then I turn over and ask Angel, "Do you think this is my punishment for having sex and getting pregnant before marriage?"

She lies next to me. "Oh My God, Jen, how can you even think this is your fault?"

I shrug my shoulders. "I keep thinking that we all pay for our sins one way or another. Maybe this is my payment. I'm the reason they had to die. God is angry at me because I had everything. The big house, fancy clothes, new car and the best parents anyone could have asked for. It wasn't enough; I thought I had to have more. I "had" to go behind their backs, have sex and get pregnant."

Angel takes a deep breath and I know she is making sure she's choosing her words carefully. "Jenna Lynn Kingsley, if you think this is your fault, you're a damn fool! I know you and I have different beliefs when it comes to God, but in this situation, neither my God nor your God would ever punish a person by taking every living relative away. He would not do that just because you decided to have a little roll in the hay. Sex is natural Jen, look Adam and Eve. They did it. God knew then that we would never be perfect here on Earth. We both know hundreds of people in school who did the deed and they still have living parents. Now, I understand you're hurt and angry, but I won't let you condemn yourself." I guess she's right but, WHY do I feel so empty?

"I know what you need Jenna. Get up and let's go for a walk."

I'm not ready to hit the beach yet, but I really need to get out of here. "Okay, let me pee, and we can take a walk."

She rolls her eyes and says, "Pee again? You made me go with you on the ferry 8 miles back. How can you pee so much?"

I laugh and tell her, "Pregnant Angel. Remember? I will pee every twenty minutes for the next few months." Angel shakes her head and squeals out "I'm never getting pregnant!" I think yeah right, famous last words of a fool.

After collecting the urns we make our way along the beach to the special place Mom found a few years ago and was in love with. She would always sit there and watch the sunset. By the time we reach that spot, the sun is on its way down. I open the box and freeze. Angel rubs my arm and asks, "What's wrong Jen?"

"This is it Angel." I begin to sob. "When I release their ashes, they will be gone forever. I'm not ready to let them go. Not now. Not ever."

Angel wraps her arms around me and holds me tight. "They will never be gone from your heart and mind, Jenna."

I know she's trying to make me feel better. It just feels so final. As I begin to spread the ashes, the wind decides to blow taking them farther out. "Why God? Why now? Why me? Why them?" The wind stops and I feel sprinkles falling. My sobs quickly turn to anger. Like taking them at the worst possible time in my life wasn't enough. Now he is going to make it rain? I am now screaming, "I am so mad at YOU! They say you are a forgiving God, but I mess up one time, ONE damn time, and you take everything from me! I'm sorry, okay? I'm so frickin sorry! Is that what you wanted? Is it? I didn't do this on purpose. I didn't want to give him my virginity. I wanted my parents to be proud of me. I didn't mean to let them down." I fall to my knees and cry until there are no more tears.

Angel breaks my thoughts when she tells me, "Feel better now, kiddo?"

I look up and tell her, "No Angel, I don't feel better. I'll never feel better. I'm sad, I'm mad. NO, I am fucking angry as Hell! I need them, Angel. I can't live in this world alone. I am only seventeen. I want my mom and dad to watch me graduate. I want my mom there to watch me give birth. I need them here with me Angel. "

"It's okay to be angry Jenna. It's okay to scream, and it's okay to hurt. Now let's get one thing straight right here. It's not okay to blame yourself. This is not your fault. This is not a punishment. This is fucking LIFE! You have always had the best. Your parents did everything in their power to give you the world. They taught you to love and trust, and that's what you did. You trusted that person you loved and you got pregnant, so what?" I want so much to believe her. How can I live is this was my fault? "It was an accident Jenna. They were in the wrong place at the wrong time. Please promise me that you won't do anything to yourself or the baby. Please?"

I look at her with such confusion. Can she hear my thoughts? Did I say it out loud and didn't realize it? "How did you know, Angel?"

"Let's get back to the house and get you fed, then we can talk. You haven't eaten anything all day. Remember that's my godchild you're carrying in there." I agree, however I'm not hungry. Just the thought of food makes me want to hurl. As we walk back to the house I remember we don't have any food there.

"We can go for a burger and fries, or call and have pizza delivered?" Angel can live on fast food; her mother was never very good in the kitchen. That's why she always shows up at my house around dinner time. My mom could cook. Her mother made sure of that because Grams' favorite saying was, *"the way to a man's heart is through his stomach."* There must be some truth to the saying. Dad always told Mom that he married her for her beauty and her cooking.

While we are eating our pizza, Angel begins her questioning. I knew they were going to start, but I am not sure I am ready for them.

"What's his name Jen?" Angel and her questions began.

"Justin."

"Oh my God, girl. Tell me it's not Justin the band nerd?"

I roll my eyes and yell, "Hell no! He doesn't go to our school, Angel."

Now comes twenty questions. "What school does he go to?"

Should I make up something or tell the truth? I decide the truth is better. "He doesn't go to school. He's well... Older."

Now I wait for that to sink in. "How much older are we talking about?" I take a deep breath. "He's twenty-one."

I know she is about to blow so I prepare myself. "Twenty-one? Jenna, have you lost your fucking mind? Does he know about the baby? Is he going to marry you? Will he at least help you support it?"

How do I answer questions that I don't have the answer to? "No he doesn't know. You're the only one who knows. We never talked about marriage. And he has a job, he works away a lot." God I don't want to talk about this.

"Where did you meet him?"

Time to stop her I had enough. I am here to mourn my parents. "At the mall. Now are you going to drill me all night? I'm really exhausted and ready for a hot shower."

Hopefully she buys my crap because I am not ready to discuss this subject. I need to talk to Justin but he hasn't answered the phone all week. "Sure, I'll let you slide, but only because you've had a long day."

Thank God, but I know it's not over with. Angel never gives up that easy. "Good night Angel and thank you for everything. I don't know what I would do without you."

We get up early the next morning and head back to Houston. I am not sure I am ready to be alone. I really don't have a choice now. I take a quick shower and throw my clothes in my backpack. Angel is already in the car so I lock up and set the alarm. Now I am leaving my parents behind once again. I have to be strong they say. How strong can I be at seventeen? I never had to be strong. I always had my parents to lean on.

Our drive back to Houston seemed a lot shorter than the trip there. We talked a lot about what we are going to do during the summer. I know there will be things I can't do but I'm okay with that. I have to think before I do things now. I need to see a doctor soon to see what I am allowed to do. Angel and I both put in applications at the mall before the end of school. She thinks it will be cool and we could meet some fine guys. Now what guy wants to look at a pregnant seventeen year old?

Thinking about being alone makes me sick. I am so afraid of being home alone. It's going to be so different from now on. I'm not sure what to do from here. I never had to make a decision like this before. Where do I start? Will I be able to stay home alone and not scare myself when I hear things at night? I guess I will have to since I have no choice. I am alone in this big old world.

Chapter 2

Coach Donavan would have my ass if he knew that I was out past midnight drinking, and banging another cheerleader. The last time I got caught with Amanda, he had me doing drills until I couldn't move. I was really bad off then. Fucking anyone to get Leah out of my head was all I could think about. Coach tried to get me to seek help after I caught my now ex-wife, Leah, with my former roommate, Noah. I wanted so much to blame it all on Noah. He and I got really close our freshman year here at LSU. I always thought we would have each other's back. Sleeping with my wife is not having my back. I drug him out of my bed by his hair and began slamming his head on the floor. I stopped cold when I heard Leah screaming, "Stop please, Bryson. Please, I love him." I knew then she was to blame as much as he was.

I slowly got off of him and snatched my gym bag from the closet. I never turned to look at her, but told her I was leaving and would return tomorrow. The last thing I wanted to see was either of their faces. I also told her she needed to get whatever she wanted out of my house tonight. I never wanted to see her again outside of divorce court.

That was the day I swore off love. I will never let any woman, besides my mother, near my heart again. Find them, Fuck them, Forget them, is my new motto. Women can take it or leave. I can care less what they think of me. I'm here at LSU to play football and finish getting my degree in Engineering. If you want to count fucking every girl I can along the way, be my guest. One thing is for sure. Falling in love again is not going to happen.

I know I will pay a price for the shots I do tonight. It is one hell of a party, and I need the escape. It seems my best friend, Ethan always throws a wild ass party on the weekends. I needed a break from my studies and football, so getting me here tonight took very little persuasion. After three shots I go on a hunt to see what, or should I say who, I could find to dip my wanting cock into. I see a few faces I recognize, so I give them a nod and one of my famous half smiles.

I spot Ramie in the living room and make my way towards her. Ramie is Ethan's younger cousin. We all grew up together. She's here for her freshman year. Ethan has warned me to stay away. So she is definitely off limits. Flirting with her, and watching her face blush is so amusing to me. Ramie has gorgeous red hair, blue eyes, big tits and the sweetest little round ass. I could ask for the moon and that girl would do what she could to bring it to me. I remember when she was such a tomboy. She would climb a tree better than most boys. Ramie would cut her hair so short if you didn't look carefully you would have thought she was a boy. Now she is all woman and turning heads. I still keep watch over her like a little sister. If these assholes think they are going to get to her without a fight ,they are wrong. Ethan and I will give them hell.

I give her a hug and spin her around quickly just to watch her face turn colors. She buries her face in my neck and gives it a little bite. God, if she only knew what that did to my dick, she would blush ten shades of darker red.

As Ramie introduces me to her friends, I raise my bottle of beer and say "Hey." A little blonde smiles and blushes, so I give her a wink. I swear I see her body shake. She puts her head down to stare at the floor and I can't help myself. I take my finger and lift her chin so that she has to look at me, "Don't hide that pretty face little darling, red really looks good on you."

She blushes again but this time Ramie smacks me on the shoulder. "Bryson stop embarrassing Amber. She is shy already and you know you could care less what color she is wearing." I give her a wink and turn to the kitchen to get another beer.

As I reach for the refrigerator door, Amanda stands in front of it. "How's it going Bry?"

"Fine Amanda. How's it going with you?" I tell her in a flat tone. I really don't give two shits about her.

"Oh my night has just gotten a whole lot better." She replies trying to use a seductive voice.

I throw my head back and laugh. All I can do is smile at the memory of her on her knees, between my legs in the locker room, sucking my cock down as far as she could. Her green eyes watering, as I face fucked her until my cum was dripping down her throat, and then laying her on the floor to fuck her. I grab a beer and head out in search of Ethan. Amanda knows I don't have a second go with anyone. It seems every time we meet up she thinks she will be the exception to the rule. Not happening!

Outside in the garage, I find Ethan passing a glass pipe to Ryan. He spots me and tries to hide it, but it's too late. Ethan and I have had this discussion more than once. He knows how I feel about that shit, and swore he would respect that I don't want to be around it. I have been there, done that. I refuse to let anyone or anything stupid like that ruin my future. I have worked my ass off in the classroom and on the field, and I will not let that shit fuck it up.

Shaking my head, I turn to walk to my truck when Ethan puts his hand on my shoulder. I shrug and he knows that he's been busted again. "Hey, bro. I'm sorry about that." I turn and stare at his bloodshot eyes.

"Really Ethan? Are you really sorry? I think you're just sorry I caught your ass again." He frowns and shakes his head no.

"I know you don't want to hear it Bryson, but I can't stop. I tried, I really tried hard. I just..." I hold my hand up in his face to stop him from the lies and excuses.

"You can stop. You just choose not to stop. You choose not to come to the meetings with me. Come on Ethan, is losing your spot on the team and failing a whole semester not enough to show you? You know that shit is fucking stupid. Dude, it has your head so fucked up that it's ruining your life. When was the last time you got a good night's sleep? Better yet when was your last decent meal?"

Ethan balls up his fists at his sides, and I step closer so we are nose to nose. "Oh you want to slam me, Ethan? You want to punch the fuck out of my face because I am trying to save your life as well as your future? Then do it dude. Take a swing. Believe me when I tell you that you're not going to like the outcome of it!" We stare in each other's eyes until he looks down. I turn and walk away, leaving him to wallow in his own shit.

Damn him, I really need to find someone hot and wet to empty my load into tonight. I head for my truck, when once again I am stopped by a small voice calling my name. I turn to see Cherie running towards me. Cherie is a pretty little thing. A little on the quiet side compared to the other cheerleaders though. When she is standing in front of me she is trying to catch her breath, so I give her a little time.

"I'm so glad I found you, Bryson. I've had enough of the party, but my ride is not ready to go. Could you please give me a ride?" I smile as my dick twitches, instantly in agreement with what's on my mind.

"Sure thing, sweetheart. I'm sure I could help a pretty little thing like you out." She rolls her eyes and says, "Cool, let me grab my purse and tell her I am leaving." As she walks away I grab my dick, willing it to hold out a few more minutes.

Ethan comes back one last time to ask me if we could possibly talk tomorrow. Preferably while we are both sober and calm. I told Ethan sure, but I am not really ready to hear the *"I can't"* and *"I'm sorry"* lines anymore. I walk away to open the door for Cherie and help her climb in the front seat. As I stroll around to my side I spot Amanda on the porch. I give her a wave as she shakes her head and turns the other way. Oh well, she knew before we did anything that I am not looking for a relationship or romance. Once is all anyone gets. She was in agreement before I ever laid her on that locker room floor. I face fucked her before I fucked her until she was screaming my name. That is how we got caught by Coach Donavan. He told me that day cheerleaders were off limits to the football team and that this was my first and last warning.

I start the truck and look over at Cherie and ask, "Where to, sweetheart?"

She shrugs her shoulders, giving me that fuck me look and says, "Wherever you want, Cowboy."

That alone should have been my cue to take her home and drive away. Oh no. Not me. Not the Bryson that is thinking with his dick. I am a man on a mission with one thing on my mind. Getting my dick into that hot, sweet pussy is all I want. Even Ryan swears she is better than any other cheerleader he has fucked.

Ryan. I am not a big fan of his for two reasons. One, he keeps supplying Ethan with that shit he does, and two, Ryan and Noah are super close. Noah has stayed out of my path after the ass whipping I gave him that night in my apartment. He would be smart to keep it that way. The month after I caught him and Leah in my bed, Leah caught him fucking Amanda in the back of his truck. Karma is a bitch, and a bitch she was. That is one day I will never forget. Leah ran into the club and threw herself in my arms. She was crying and saying how sorry she was and how she didn't really love him. I peeled her away from me and laughed saying, "You made your bed Leah, now lay in it because you will never ever lay in mine again."

Cherie's voice pulls me back to the here and now. "Why the cheesy smile, Bryson?" I hadn't realized I was smiling.

"Oh, I was just having a quick stroll down memory lane."

She laughs her little silly laugh. "Must have been one hell of a memory to make you smile like that. I haven't seen you smile like that since Leah caught Noah and Amanda in the back of his truck."

I throw my head back and laugh hard. "Well, sweetheart, that's the same memory that has me smiling now." We both laugh and I hear my jam on the radio and turn it up. We drive the rest of the way singing to the radio as Travis Tritt sings *"Here's a Quarter, Call Someone Who Cares."*

Once inside my apartment, I tell Cherie to make herself comfortable. I ask her if she wants something to drink. She shakes her head no. I catch myself some water and sit beside her on the couch. Immediately, she grabs my face and kisses me. I'm not shocked, but I pull away. Kissing is not what I brought her here for. Kissing is for relationships, and I don't do those. I grab her shirt and begin to pull it over her head. Cherie reaches behind her back and her bra comes sliding down her arms. Unzipping her jeans and pulling them down was done in record time. She pulls on my shirt and in one swift move, it's over my head and flying across the room. I reach for her little pink lace thong and rip it in two. Placing one finger between her wet pussy, I find she is dripping. She smiles, but never stops me when I add a second finger. I push deeper inside her pussy. She closes her eyes and moans as I work them in a circular motion. Just before I add the third finger, I put a little pressure on her clit. She bucks her hips and begins to ride my fingers. At that moment, I know I can have her cum on my fingers in seconds. A little more pressure on her clit and she's screaming.

I remove my fingers and make quick work of losing my jeans. Within seconds I have her flipped over the back of the sofa. I put my mouth to her ear and tell her, "This is a one-time deal Cherie. I won't call you tomorrow. I won't take you to dinner. Most of all I won't be buried balls deep inside you again after tonight."

She gets what I am saying and turns her head to see that I'm serious. "Fuck me, Cowboy! Fuck me like your life depends on it, and don't be gentle!" Bam. Just the words I want to hear. I tear open the rubber from my back pocket and roll it on my aching cock. I grab her hair and give it a tug, as I enter her wet pussy in one swift hard move. I hear her moan as I pull out and shove it in again and again. She matches my rhythm and begins shouting, "Right there Bryson. Fuck me harder. Harder, Bryson! I'm going to cum. Don't stop!" I continue my pumping and pull her hair, telling her, "Let it go, NOW!" She clamps down on my dick and I feel her body shake as she cums. I give a few more hard pumps, and empty myself inside her. I pull out, grabbing my jeans and shirt as I head down the hall. I don't do the talking thing after sex. After I turn the shower on to let it warm up, I dispose of the condom and grab a towel.

After a few minutes in the shower, I dry off and dress. I smile at myself in the mirror before opening the door. When I return to the living room I see a note on the table. I pick it up and read, *"Thanks Cowboy. See ya around. C."* Well, that was one of the easiest fucks I've ever had. Most want me to bring them home or try the "can you hold me just a minute" routine. But hey, I wish they would all just see themselves out while I'm in the shower. I know I'm a dick, but you only get to fuck me once and that happened a year ago. My ex-wife was the last person I allowed to fuck me. Now it's my turn to do the fucking.

Chapter 3

Jenna

The doorbell rings, and I expect to see Angel since she refuses to leave me alone. She's afraid I will try taking my life. I made a promise and swore I wouldn't try anything stupid. That would mean I would be dammed to Hell and would never be able to see my parents again. From now on I have to make all the right choices so I can guarantee my spot in heaven with my parents. But is there even a guarantee?

Upon opening the door, I am greeted by a smiling woman holding a briefcase. She shows me an I.D. and introduces herself as Mrs. Kathie Hickman with Social Services. I'm not sure what she's here for, but I invite her in. I show her to the living room and we sit. After pulling paperwork from her briefcase she begins telling me that my life, that I thought couldn't get any worse at this point, has just reached another level on the crappy scale. It's now worse than I could have ever imagined.

"Jenna, I have some news for you. I know you are not going to like it. I need you to understand I am only doing my job." I wish she would just tell me already. She is making me nervous.

"Okay, just tell me what you have to say. I don't think my life can get any worse than it is now." I don't care for the way she is looking at me. She has the same look as the police officer that gave me the news on my parents.

"Jenna, due to the fact you are only seventeen and without a living parent or relative, you are now a ward of the State of Texas." Oh my God.

"Mrs. Hickman, what are you saying? What does this mean?"

"It means you have to come with me. I will place you in a foster home until you're of legal age."

"You mean I have to leave my home? This is the only home I have ever known. There has to be something you can do. Please I can't just go live with strangers. My life is here. Don't take me away from my home, it's all I have left." I have to think of something. I can't let her take me away.

"Believe me, Jenna. If I could, I would. There is no other option unless you have a living relative. From what I have gathered there is none. I know this will be hard for you Jenna. Let's look on the bright side. It's only like 3 or so months. It will fly by you will see." ONLY THREE MONTHS? Is this woman for real? I have to call Angel. She will know what to do.

"Nothing in my life is bright anymore, Mrs. Hickman." What's next?

"Jenna, I need you to pack a bag now so we can go." FUCK MY LIFE!

"I have my own car. I can follow you. I will need my car for cheer practice over the summer." At least I could still see my friends and go shopping.

"I'm sorry Jenna, but your car and insurance is under your father's name. It will have to stay parked until you are of legal age. Same with the house and your parent's bank accounts." Oh my God. What am I going to do now? I have to text Angel.

I snatch my phone from my purse and send a quick text to Angel.

- GET HERE NOW!!!

- OMW what's up?

- HURRY 911!!

Mrs. Hickman asks if I need her to help me pack. I tell her no, that I am capable of packing myself. After I go into my room and lock my door, I pace my room trying to think of what to do? Who do I call, and how do I stop all this? Nothing comes to mind.

I hear banging on my door, and Angel yells, "Open the damn door Jenna!" I swing open the door and throw my arms around her neck.

"Oh, my God, Angel! Don't let her take me, please. I can't go live with people I don't know! I can't even drive my car anymore. Angel, please! Please you have to help me!"

Angel squeezes my body and tries to calm me. "Okay, Jenna. Take deep breaths. We are going to go down and see what options you have. You're getting ahead of yourself. I need you to just calm down before we talk to Miss Fancy Pants in the living room." I do as she says and take a few deep breaths, trying to hold it together.

Kathie explains everything in detail again while we hang on to every word. By law there is nothing I can do. She goes on to say that at the age of eighteen everything my parents own will be all mine. However, for now all will remain frozen. *Lord, why does life have to be so complicated?*

I consider telling her about the baby but decide to wait. I still haven't been able to get in touch with Justin. He hasn't returned any of my calls or texts. I leave messages, and pray nothing is wrong.

Mrs. Leigh Ann, Angel's mom, has joined us and asked Kathie to give me two hours to get things together, and prepare the house to be left for the next three months. Kathie agrees and says she will return in two hours, or I can text her if we finish before then. While Angel cleans out the refrigerator and loads the dishwasher, Mrs. Leigh Ann goes through Mom's desk to get all household bills together. We need to take care of them so things don't get disconnected. I have never paid a bill in my life, I know nothing about it. But I do have money in the checking account Daddy insisted I have, along with a savings account. Daddy was trying to teach me how to manage my money, so he always deposited it, whether it was needed or not. It should keep me for a few months. I know he has $25,000.00 in the safe that he always kept on hand in case of an emergency. Daddy was always afraid we would have an emergency and the ATM's would be out. Mom didn't like him keeping that much in the safe; she says it was too risky.

When we are finished, we have discovered that the house and cars are paid off. It looks like Daddy had paid off everything when he sold his business. So, all in all, it's just a few household bills that need to be paid. *I can do that, I hope.*

After I have everything packed and ready to go, I walk through the house to make sure all is secured. The timers are set so that the a few lights will come on and go off at certain times to keep people from knowing that no one is home. It was something Daddy insisted we needed, beings we all had busy lives. I walk into their room and the peace I feel is like no other feeling I've had in the past week. On Mom's dresser, I spot the photo of them on their 25th wedding anniversary. I take it down carefully, and hold it to my chest. I am definitely taking this with me. Before I leave their room, I flush their toilet and closed the lid (something Mrs. Leigh says is a must).

Once down stairs, I meet up with Angel and her mom and walk into their open arms. I cry and thank them so much for all they have done for me. I really would not have known what to do. They promise to keep in touch. and tell me that I can come for visits anytime. I thank them once again and the doorbell rings. It's time, and I'm not ready. I don't want to go. This is my home. I need to stay here. *Why God? Why me? Why now?*

After we walk out to put my bags in Mrs. Hickman's car, Angel grabs me in a hug and we both begin to cry again. I'm not ready to say good-bye. "It's only three months. We can do this", she whispers in my ear.

I try to give a smile and say, "Only three months."

I get in the car and tell her I will call her everyday so we can hang out until school starts again. Kathie says we must go now. I hug her once more and close the door. The tears are now pouring, and I can't stop them. Having to say goodbye to my life as I've known it seems like the end of the world. But if there is one thing in life I have learned in all this is, it is DO NOT ASK "WHAT'S NEXT?" You may not like the answer.

As Mrs. Hickman and I hit the interstate heading west, I lay my seat back and try to clear my mind, not sure of what is in store for me. Besides a sleepover with Angel or our family vacations, I have never been away from home. I am trying to be as positive about this as I can. I just hope these three months fly by.

I must have dozed off when I feel the car stop and the engine die. I sit up and see we are in someone's driveway. I don't recognize the neighborhood so I ask where we are and she replies with Sequin. *Oh my God, is she serious right now? Small Town, USA?* Positive, Jenna. Positive.

"I know this is hard for you, Jenna, but it's only three months, honey. You will see. They will go by so fast, and you will be home before you know it." Kathie is really sweet and I know she is trying to sympathize with me, but she has no clue what I'm going through.

"Thanks, Kathie. I've got this!" We walk to the front door, and she knocks and knocks.

Finally, the door flies open and a teenage boy answers it. If I had to guess his age I would say twelve or so. He looks me up and down and turns to Kathie and glares at her. Whoa. He looks pissed at her.

"What is wrong with you, Caden?" He must be a foster child here too. He is not very respectful. I try to break the glare and say, "Hi." He gives me a creepy look.

"You must be the new rich girl they said was coming. Your parents are dead, right?"

"Stop it, Caden. What is wrong with you? That was rude and hurtful. Now you apologize to Jenna Now!" Kathie looks like she is about to spit fire.

"What are you yelling at me for? That's what they told me."

That's it, I have had enough and I want to go home now. I turn and head for the car. "Where is your mom, Caden?" Kathie looks around him.

"SHE'S. NOT. MY. MOM! Don't you ever call her that again! I have a mom that loves me. If you would just get them to release her from jail, I could go home."

Oh nice. His mother is in jail, and he looks like he has raised himself. Yay me. You only have three months, Jenna. Three little months. Kathie comes to meet me at the car and explains that he's angry at the world, and refuses to talk to the councilors to help him cope. He has sisters, but they are all split up in the system. My heart aches for him, but he needs to be considerate of others, too. I understand his pain. I want my mother too, but at least he has hope that one day she will be released and they will be together again. I don't have that hope to hold onto. *I want to go home.*

I grab my bags from the car and tell her. "It's okay. I can do this for three months. I don't have a choice. I want to be back at my school. This is going to be my senior year. I will pay Angel's gas to come get me if I have to. I will not go to school in this hick town." She just smiles at me like I am speaking another language or something.

Once inside, Caden comes from the back of the house, and says Louise is coming. I take-in the living room and kitchen. It's a lot smaller than I am used to, but I will live. I just hope the cleaning lady comes soon.

Minutes later a little grey haired lady comes in and introduces herself to me. "Hi, I'm Louise. You must be Jennifer?"

I shake my head. "Jenna. My name is Jenna." *Who is this woman? Is she the grandmother or the foster mother? I hope it's not the later.*

"Jenna this is Louise, she is your new foster mother. She has fostered many of our children over the years." Oh great, looks like shopping at the mall is totally out of the question. This little old lady doesn't look like she leaves the bed very often, much less the house.

"Louise, if you don't mind could you show Jenna to her room?" Yay, I get to see my room. My sanctuary. My home away from home.

She leads us down a short hallway and points to the third door on the right. "This is your room. It's across from mine. I like to keep the girls close so I can keep an eye on them. I will warn you I sleep very light, and I hear everything. Don't go trying any hanky panky in my house, young lady."

Whoa, Grandma Jones. Hanky Panky with whom? Caden, the little rude ass kid with the bad hair? *Oh, this is going to be a long three months*. I open the door and, believe me when I tell you, I was not even close to being prepared to see what's before me.

This room is smaller than my closet at home, and has three twin beds, which means I have to share my private space.

"You are the only girl for now, but this is subject to change at any time." Oh thank God, I hope it stays that way until I'm gone. Kathie asks if I want her to help me unpack, and I let her know, once more, that I am very capable of unpacking my own bags. I walk her out to her car and thank her for all she's done for me. She gives me a hug and says she will check in on me from time to time. I can't hold back the tears any longer. Kathie takes me in her arms and lets me cry it out.

"Thank you, Mrs. Hickman. I am sorry you had to see me like this, but I couldn't hold out any longer. I really am trying to be strong." She gives me a smile and I walk to the house.

Once back in my room, I take out my phone and send a quick text to Angel.

**Hey biotch.

*Hey Boo how's it going?

**Okay, I guess

*Where are you?

**You're not going to believe me when I tell you

*Really? Try me!

**Sequin

*NO FUCKING WAY!!

**Yes way! It totally sucks too.

*That's like an hour away Jen:(

  **Yes I know. I am totally bummed and hate being so far from home.

*We won't be able to hang out every day.

**I know don't remind me.

**TTYL I have to unpack.

*Love ya, Boo

**Love ya back Toots.

I put my earphones in and start my playlist. Unpacking in this matchbox they call a room feels so strange. I turn to get hangers and I am spooked by Caden standing in my doorway, just staring at me. "You scared the shit out of me, Caden. Why are you in my room without permission? You need to learn to knock. My room is my personal space and no one should invade it without asking." He starts laughing and laughing. He gets louder and I wonder what is it that I said that was so funny.

Finally he stops and says. "Here you have no personal space, rich girl. No one knocks or ask to enter your space. Check your door knobs. No one has locks in this hellhole." I check the knob. No locks. Surely there is one on the bathroom door? I check it out and see there is none there either. Well, we will have to do something about this shit. I will not take a shit or shower without a lock on the door. This has to be against the law. Everyone has a right to privacy. I think it's time to have a little talk with Mrs. Louise and demand that locks be put on our doors.

I go in search of Louise, only to find her at the kitchen table with a lit cigarette and cheap bottle of wine. Oh, things are really going to have to change. I will not have my clothes and hair smelling like an ashtray, not to mention my lungs. We have rights here, and it's time someone let them know it.

Before I get my first word out, I hear Caden calling for me. "Jenna, can you come see a minute, please?" The please really lets me know it may be important. I go back to my room, and he closes the door behind me.

I raise my eyebrow and he says. "Calm down, rich girl. You're not my type. I just want to give you a little heads up on how things go around here before you go making trouble for all of us."

Ha, I'm not his type? Why, because I have some class or maybe I have more balls than he does? "Louise and Clay are assholes. They couldn't care less about anyone but themselves and the bottle. She will sit her ass at that kitchen table and drink until he gets home. Drunk and ready to fight, they will scream and yell at each other and whoever else comes into view. He will cuss a lot, and she will throw her empty bottles at him. He will come find one, if not all of us, to fight with. He will throw us around and blame us all for things she doesn't do. When he has enough, he will go in his room and pass out. She will follow him and all will be quiet until 5 a.m."

Oh my God, is he serious? Is this really how other people live? Why would anyone put children here? He has to be exaggerating. This can't be possible. I hold my stomach and sink to the floor, wondering what they're doing here. What am I going to do? I can't let him hit me, or throw me around. I have to protect my baby.

"Caden, why haven't you told Kathie? I'm sure she would take you away from here."

He gives me a pissed off look. "Pssh, why would I want to leave here? This is a walk in the park compared to the last three homes I have been in. Believe me, the last house I was in was a lot worse. The dad held a gun to our heads and made us beg him not to pull the trigger. It wasn't until one of the boys got arrested for stealing food at a local Mini Mart that anything happened. The police called OCS in and questioned him. He told them he was stealing the food to feed all the foster kids in the home. They finally investigated it and closed them down, placing all of us in different homes. So, don't jump to judge this one as being the worst. It really is better than some."

Jesus Christ, this kid has been through some shit no one should have to go through. How can they give children to these people? Do they not check them out before handing over innocent children? Do they not check on them daily?

Bang. I hear the door slam and my eyes go wide. "Caden, please. I can't let him hit me or throw me around, I can't." I hold my stomach tighter, and look for a place to hide.

"Just stay put. He doesn't know you're here yet, so I'll take it all tonight, but you will owe me, rich girl."

I will do anything he wants. "You got it, Caden. Anything, I promise. Just don't let him hit me."

The yelling begins. I try to cover my ears but that does nothing. The cussing and glass breaking starts and gets louder. I'm not sure what is going on. I pull my phone from the bed, not sure what to do with it. I don't want it to make any noise and tip him off that I am here, so I turn it on vibrate and stare at my screen saver. It's a picture of me, Mom, and Dad in Italy. It was our Christmas vacation. We were all smiling and happy. I cry and pray. I just want to go home. I can't live like this. I had everything. How did I get here?

Chapter 4

Waking up at 7:00 a.m. on a Sunday morning to a ringing phone is enough to piss me the fuck off. "Hello, this better be fucking important. Oops. Sorry, Mom."

I love my mother to death, but dammit, 7:00 a.m.? Really? Can't she wait and call me after church? I sit here with the phone to my ear. I have to listen to the same shit she lectured me on last Sunday. I know I should go to church. I know I need God in my life. But, I don't think he wants me there with the hangover I have today. My head feels like it will explode at any minute.

"I know, Mom. I will try to catch a mass later today. I'm just not feeling well this morning and wanted to catch up on some sleep." Damn do women ever stop bitching? "Yes, Mom, I know. Yes, I promise I will come for a couple of weeks once coach releases us. Look, Mom, can I call you later? I have another call coming in. I love you, Mom. Bye."

"Hello?" It's damn Grand Central Station at seven fucking a.m. in the mother fucking morning. Don't people fucking sleep?

I hear the soft voice of Ramie, "Hey sexy." I smile knowing she is only joking, and nothing will ever come out of it.

"Yes, Sweetpea. What can I do for you?" I sit and listen to her breathe for a few seconds and wonder if she's okay.

"I'm really worried about Ethan."

I sit straight up at the mention of his name, "What's wrong Ramie? Did something happen to Ethan? Is he ok?"

She sighs, "No, nothing really bad happened. I'm not sure what happened between you and Ethan last night. After you left, he came in and threw everyone out. He broke the t.v. and tried to fight some big guy I don't even think he knew. We had to pull them apart. I don't like the anger he showed. It was like it was someone else in his body. I know that sounds stupid. I am not used to Ethan being mean like that."

Fucking meth head can't control his shit. I knew this was coming again. Same shit as last time. "Ramie, honey, stay in your room and just chill. I will be there later to deal with him. Oh, and if Ryan should come by, tell him Ethan is not in and call me." It's time to get Ryan out of Ethan's life. I can see an ass whipping in his near future.

"Okay Bry, thank you. I am really sorry for calling so early. I didn't know what else to do. Calling Nanny Patty is the last thing I wanted to do with her health and all. You are the only other person I know that can talk to him. I know he won't listen to me."

She's right Patty is not well enough to deal with his shit right now. "You did the right thing calling me. I will get there as soon as I can. Bye, Sweetheart."

It's time to put my foot in his ass. I love my friend like the brother I never had, but he's gone too far this time. Fuck, I guess staying in bed until noon is shot to shit now. It's going to be a long fucking day. Isn't Sunday supposed to be a day of rest?

I stumble out of bed and head to the bathroom. I wash my face and brush my teeth. My stomach grumbles and I try to remember my last good home cooked breakfast. Oh, that's easy. The last time I was home. My mom is kick ass in the kitchen. Damn, I miss home. I need to make friends with some of these Cajun girls. I'm sure I could get a good home cooked meal in trade for a little romp in the hay. I grab a breakfast shake and head to the garage. I think I will take the Harley out today. There's just something about the wind in my face that helps clear my head. There's a sense of freedom, and Lord knows I need a clear head to go deal with Ethan. *God, please give me the strength to deal with this mess.*

I am in the twelve step program for my drug use, so I know my higher power. I know I am nothing without him. I also know that through him all things are possible. Today, I will have to call on him to help me because my best friend is as stubborn as a mule. I have made up my mind that if he doesn't admit his problem and get help, I am done. I will walk away from him and never turn back. I have tried everything to get him to stop, so it's time for some tough love.

I pull in the driveway, and there is Noah's truck. The last person I need to see is fucking Noah. I can't deal with him on this crazy ass morning. I walk in the house without knocking, like I always do. It's quiet, and no one is around. I head to the rooms at the back of the house.

I hear Ramie yell, "NO! Get off me before I scream, Noah." I fly to her door to find it locked, so I give it a hit with my shoulder and it swings open. There is Noah, straddling her. He has her hands trapped above her head. I see red and charge his ass. We tumble to floor, and I wrap my hands around his throat. I am going to enjoy watching this mother fucker take his last breath. I want to see his eyes pop out of his head. His journey to hell to meet the devil will be my pleasure. Ramie screams and I turn to see what's wrong. She's begging me to stop. I loosen my hold and turn back to him.

"This is your lucky fucking day, Noah. I am going to punch you and then I am going to let you go. You will never come within 100 feet of Ramie again. Do you understand me?" He nods his head, and like I promised, I punch him square in his face and let go. He takes off from the room coughing and spitting, just as Ethan is entering the room.

"What the hell is going on in here?" I glare at him and let him in on what happened. I refuse to hold anything back. It's time for him to face reality.

"If you can't stay off that shit long enough to protect Ramie, then I will take her home with me. You took on the responsibility of protecting her. You promised her mama you would not let anything happen to her. Yet, I come in on that son of a bitch about to rape her while you're passed the fuck out. You're doing so much shit you don't know which way is up anymore. You're the next one on my list Ethan. I am at the end of my rope. You have to make a choice right here, right now. If you can't man the fuck up and get off all the bullshit. I am taking Ramie and walking out that door. When I do, I never want to see you again. You get me, Ethan?"

He looks from me to Ramie who is balled up in a fetal position crying. She is scared out of her mind. He goes over to her, pulls her into his lap, and rocks her. My heart breaks for her. She is like a baby sister to me. He consoles her while I pace the floor. He finally speaks, and I stop dead in my tracks as the words roll off his tongue.

"I'm done. I will never touch that shit again. I'm ready, Bryson. I want help. I want to go to the meetings. I want the treatment." When his eyes reach mine, I see the tears rolling down his face and I know he's serious. "I want my life back. I want what you got, Bryson. I want to be in the top of my class again. I want to be the man on the field again." Thank God, something finally got through that thick ass skull of his.

"Awesome, dude! Meeting tomorrow night. I'll pick you up at 6:30. It's the first step. Now, for step two. Get them lowlife's out of your life. Pick up your phone and text them that you no longer want them around you or your house. That you will no longer be using anything they have to offer." He walks off, and I think I have pissed him off. I gear up for round two. I will fight him if I have to.

He picks up his phone from the bedside table and begins to text. When he is done, he hands me the phone so I can read it. A sigh of relief comes from my chest, and I smile. "I am so fucking proud of you right now, dude. I can't even explain the feeling, man. Just know I love you and I am here for you through thick and thin. I will stand by you." I pull him in for a bro hug and give him a slap on the back. "Now, let's go see about Red and make sure that fucktard didn't hurt her. I swear if he hurt one hair on her head, he better give his soul to God because his slimy ass is mine."

When Ethan and I go to the bedroom, Ramie is gone. I search the bathroom and the closet, and she is nowhere to be found. I turn to Ethan and tell him she's not there. We both take off for the living room, and smell bacon coming from the kitchen. Oh man, my stomach does a flip when I walk in. There she is with three plates overflowing with eggs, grits, bacon and toast. Damn, a man can get used to this. I sure hope it tastes as good as it smells. Did I mention I love

Cajun cooking? My day seems to be getting better and better!

We eat breakfast and talk to Ramie, making sure she's okay. She assures me that he had just straddled her when I walked in. He had not violated her. She says she's not traumatized and refuses to see a counselor. I make sure she understands I am always here for her and hope she can trust me.

"Trust you? You're my fucking hero Bryson. I don't even want to imagine what would have happened to me had you not showed up when you did." I don't want to think about it. I let her know it was my pleasure to punch that dickhead again and would do it more if need be.

Ethan and I decide to take a ride on our bikes and see if we can get our shit together. Finals are coming up, so we will both be out of the loop for a while. I thank Ramie and give her a big bear hug and a wet kiss on the cheek.

Freedom, here we come!

Chapter 5

Jenna

The yelling continues and my body is just numb. My mind is trying to make sense of what's going on. I cry because I want my daddy. I want to go home. Bang. The door across the hall slams. Bang. It slams again, and then all is quiet. I hear a soft tap on my door but I can't move. I hold my breath as the door opens and I see Caden. I sigh and run to him. Blood is leaking from his nose and mouth. "God, Caden! Did he do this to you? Is this what happens every day?" I snatch a shirt from my bed and try to wipe off some of the blood. I need to see what damage has been done. He flinches and pulls away.

"Not every day. I usually make sure I am out in the woods, or in my room until he's in bed. Tonight I stayed only to protect you." He looks down at my belly and I wonder if he knows? Should I tell him? He saved me and my baby tonight. I can't let him keep doing that. I just don't know what to do. I can't even think right now.

My stomach chooses this time to growl. I realize I haven't eaten all day. "What do we eat around here, Caden?"

He shakes his head. "She doesn't cook, and that's what they fight over most nights. In the freezer, they have frozen pizzas or t.v. dinners. Sometimes we have cold cuts to make sandwiches. Their son, Bryan, works at Market Basket, so he brings things home that we can cook on our own."

Geez, it gets worse by the minute. How can I live on cold cuts and frozen dinners? My baby needs healthy food. Think, Jenna. how you can change things?

"What happens if we wake them when we go to the kitchen to prepare it?" He rolls his eyes.

"Nah, once they hit the bed they are out until the alarm goes off at 5 a.m."

Okay, I can live with that. I will need to get to this Bryan person. Hopefully, he can get a few things for me at the grocery store. Thank God mom made me help her around the kitchen, and insisted I learn to cook. She gave me many of Gammy's secret family recipes. They have been passed down for many generations. I think if I can talk Louise into letting me prepare dinner. I could possibly put a stop to some of the arguments. Maybe we can have a normal life here. If he comes home to a nice home cooked meal, maybe he won't stop and get drunk before coming home. It's worth a try. I will ask Caden what he thinks.

We heat up a couple of pizzas and sit down to eat. Caden eats like it's his last meal. This must be the only thing he has eaten all day. I hear the front door open and I freeze. "It's only Bryan. He's cool." I let the breath I'm holding go and see a tall, somewhat good looking man walk into the kitchen with a bag of groceries.

"Who's your friend?"

Caden shakes his head, "Not my friend, she's our foster sister, Bro." Now it's his turn to shake his head.

"When the hell are they going to learn to stop sending females to this hellhole?" What is that suppose to mean? Do they dislike girls? Has something happened?

"That's the same thing I was thinking when I laid eyes on rich girl here. She's not only eye candy, but she's also loaded. Louise is going to hate her, and Clay is going to stay sober more. Life around here is about to suck ass dude."

Bryan glares at him and pops him behind his head. "Watch your mouth around they lady, dude."

"Can you both stop talking about me like I'm not here? I can hear y'all, you know?"

Caden laughs. "Sorry rich girl. This is Bryan, the real son I told you about. He's the reason we eat around here."

I turn to Bryan and give him my hand, "Jenna Kingsley. So nice to meet you, Bryan." He shakes my hand.

"Welcome to Hell, Shorty. Stay out of sight, hang low, and maybe we can keep you more than a week." I wish I understood what they meant, but then again, I'm afraid to find out.

"Bryan, Caden told me you can get groceries from where you work? If I give you money and a list, do you think you can get them for me?"

A big smile creeps up on his face, "Sure, rich girl. You buying the grub around here will allow me to pocket some of the money I work for. Carrying the load for you kids is getting pretty old. Not sure why I have to pay for shit my parents do around here. Of course, I can't let you all starve. Make the list and I'll pick it up tomorrow. I work the early shift tomorrow, so I will need it tonight."

I decide on gumbo, so I check the cabinets and freezer to see what I will need to buy. When I complete my list I get the money and tap, on Bryan's door. That was the easy part of my plan. Now we have to keep our fingers crossed that Louise will allow me to cook in her kitchen.

That night, sleep just won't come with the million things I have running through my head. Finding a solution to the problems here is my main concern. Caden needs some peace until he can reunite with his mother and siblings. The alarm goes off in the room across the hall and I panic. I pray silently that Clay doesn't open my door. After a few minutes, I hear him in the kitchen. I smell fresh brewed coffee. God, I wish I could have a tall glass of my mom's fabulous coffee milk. The things I always took for granted are now hitting home for me. I know I need to be thankful for what I have and really not worry about those I can't have anymore.

I bury my face in my pillow and cry. I think my hormones are whacked. I haven't cried this much in my whole life. I miss my parents so much. I wish I could have them here for one more day. I swear I would shower their faces with kisses and I would say "I love you" a million times. I would tell them how much I appreciate them and all they did for me. *God, why didn't I tell them when I had the chance?*

After I hear the front door close, I take a deep breath and begin to get dressed in order to go find something to eat. When I round the corner, Louise is sitting at the table smoking again. Ugh, the smell is God awful. She turns to look at me so I smile and say, "Good morning."

She rolls her eyes and says, "Good morning, Jennifer." I decide to choose my battles and leave it alone. I go through the refrigerator to find breakfast. I am shocked when Louise says, "help yourself to whatever you can find." Then she goes off to her bedroom. Thank God. That smoke is making me sick. I dart to the bathroom and make it just in time to empty my stomach. Oh please God, not now. Morning sickness is the last thing I need. I brush my teeth and put a cool rag on my throat.

Returning to the kitchen, I pull out a few things to make breakfast. Eggs, sausage, and homemade biscuits are all I can throw together for now. As I am taking the biscuits out of the oven, Caden and Bryan enter the kitchen. They look at each other and give a high five. I laugh and put out all the food. They eat like cavemen. It's a good thing my stomach refuses to let me eat. That reminds me, I need to add crackers and sprite to the grocery list. Mom always said that's the only thing to calm an upset stomach.

Bryan brings his plate to the sink. "Thanks for the grub, rich girl. I can't remember the last time I had a cooked breakfast besides Mc Donald's." I smile, happy I could do something to show my appreciation for him and what he does to help us. "I have to hurry before I am late. The only good thing about going in early is I will be off early. I will see you guys when I get home."

Caden doesn't get up from the table until all the food has disappeared. He brings his plate to the sink and begins to load the dishwasher. I clear the table and wipe down the cabinets. When the kitchen is clean, he asks me if I want to take a walk so he can show me where he spends most of his time. I stare at him in disbelief, this isn't right. This child should not have to hide out every day. This is supposed to be his home. I grab my shoes and phone from my room and off we go.

We walk for a ways in silence and Caden starts talking about his mother and his sisters. He gives me the whole story as far as he can remember back. I stay quiet, and just let him talk. He really misses his sisters and hasn't seen them since they were split up. He also says he thinks his mother was pregnant when she was arrested, he doesn't know what happened to that baby, or if it is a boy or a girl. He's a very sad boy that feels all alone in this crazy world. My heart is heavy. I can't imagine having to go through a fourth of what this child has been through.

I decide I have to help him. Show him life is better than what he's seen of it. I need to find ways to bring joy to his life for the months I have here. He needs to know love. He needs to know that there are good and kind people in this world. In our conversation, I find out he has never even played an X-box or Playstation game. He's never been on a vacation or to a beach, or an amusement park. Not even a live ball game. NOTHING. It's heartbreaking, and I know I have to show him, give him, a bit of joy. But how?

It's after two when we walk back into the house. I hadn't realized we were gone so long. Hearing loud voices coming from the kitchen, Caden places himself between me and the kitchen. We listen for a bit and figure out it's Bryan and Louise. She tells him that she thinks it's best for him to stay clear of me because I'm nothing but trouble. What the hell did I do? Why would she say that? I march my ass into the kitchen and ask her. She is shocked but Bryan steps up and tries to repair the damage. He says she is only worried because he's over eighteen and I'm not, and in the past there was a girl who claimed he had tried something sexual with her. I understand, and tell Louise she has nothing to worry about with me. I only want to get through the next few months without any harm to anyone.

I go in my bedroom, and I am texting Angel to see what's going on in Houston when I hear a tap on my door.

"Come in." Bryan opens the door and says he has everything on the list and tries to give me the change. I tell him to keep it for his trouble. He also lets me know that I have the okay from Louise to cook whenever I want.

I thank him and expect him to close my door and leave, but he shuts the door, "Jenna can we talk about what you overheard earlier?" He has already explained it all, so what more is there to explain?

"I told you, I understand now. You really don't need to explain anymore. I will stay away from you and keep to myself so no one gets in trouble."

"Jenna, I lied." He takes a deep breath, and rubs his hand down his face. "I was never accused of such a thing. My father was, and I don't doubt for one minute that he did it. I just didn't want my mother to scream and mistreat you." Oh dear God. Why does everyone around here protect Clay? How could Bryan make himself look like a creep when he's not?

"Why, Bryan? Why protect him? Better yet, why protect me? You don't even know me."

He turns to look me dead in the eyes and says, "I know enough to know you're a good person. The way Caden looks up to you tells me I can trust you. That boy doesn't trust anyone. He keeps everything bottled up inside. He's been here over a year and we've had at least twenty kids through this hellhole. He didn't speak to any of them. Last night, he came to my room and said you were different from all the rest. He says you would need our help. If he can trust you after everything he's been through, then so can I. I will help you. Whatever you need, I am here."

Wow, I never would have guessed that Caden didn't talk to others. The way he let it all go today, you would think he had spoken about it many times. "Thank you, Bryan. I may need your help with things while I'm here. I can't thank you enough for getting the things I needed today." He nods and walks out. There are so many things I need. I just have to make sure I can trust him. I will start with little things, and work my way up.

I find Louise in the kitchen again, and ask her if it's okay to cook one of my mom's favorite dishes. She says I can cook whatever I want. The deal is I was to be out of sight before Clay returns from work. She also said tht after he goes to bed, I am to make sure the kitchen is cleaned. Not fully understanding why, I agree with her terms and begin making dinner.

I have the chicken and sausage cut up and seasoned, and I start to get the roux and onions to boiling. I peel all the potatoes and get them and the eggs to boiling as well. I'm making gumbo with chicken and sausage over rice with potato salad on the side. Louise continues to drink her cheap wine and smoke her nasty smelling cigarettes, while calling me Jennifer. Correcting her is useless anymore, so I just answer to it.

After all is cooked, I turn it off and let her know it's ready to eat. She nods and tells me to serve myself a bowl, and take it to my bedroom. I'm a little pissed off because I really wanted to see how Bryan and Caden would react. But, I will do as I am told to keep the peace, and take my food to my room and shut my door.

The food came out perfect, and makes me lonesome for my parents. I miss them so much. I wish they were here to taste how good this turned out. Daddy would be so proud of me. Tears begin to fall and I let them. I can't keep hoping this is all a dream. This is my new life and I have to move forward, but it doesn't stop the heartache and tears.

I hear the door slam and I freeze and wait for the screaming, but it doesn't come. I can hear talking, but can't make out what or who it is. I finish my food, and wait for the glass to start breaking, but it doesn't. After what seems like forever, I finally hear the door across the hall close and, minutes later, a tap comes on my door. I don't say anything, but the door opens slowly, and Bryan and Caden come in.

"Well, guys, how did it go?"

I watch the smiles creep up on their faces. "How did you learn to cook like that rich girl?" I laugh and tell them how my mother insisted I learn to cook.

"Where are Clay and Louise?" They look at each other and smile. Bryan finally says. "They went to bed together holding hands and kissing all the way to the room. I'm pretty sure they are honeymooning."

I smile. "Good, maybe my plan is working after all."

"Come on, Jenna. Caden and I will help with the kitchen since you cooked."

We all do the dishes and clean up the kitchen when Bryan says, "Hey, how would you like to go get an ice cream in town? I will be happy to bring y'all."

Bryan is such a sweetheart. "Okay, but I am paying. I get my purse and shoes and head to the car.

Caden is all smiles and that makes my night. "I want you both to order whatever you want, and don't worry about the price. This celebration is on me."

Chapter 6

Ethan and I ride the countryside for miles. Riding gives me some much needed head time. After vacation, I will only have one semester left. I reflect back to a discussion Leah and I had about starting a family after our college graduation. Children were one of the few things we both agreed on. We would have a girl for me and a boy for her. We always said that people say a boy for the man and a girl for the woman, but they had it backwards. Daddy spoils the girls and Mommy spoils the boys. I smile at the thought of my baby girl resting on my chest after I come home from a hard day's work. She would definitely be daddy's little princess.

Not sure why I'm smiling, because that plan is gone for good. I always wondered what I did to be fucked out of my dreams. I wanted to marry my high school sweetheart, graduate college four years later, move back to Beaumont to work as a partner with my father, and build our home on my parents' ranch so we could start our own little family. Well, here I am divorced from my wife, graduating in a few months, and going back to Beaumont to work with my father, only to become the oldest bachelor alive to live at home with Mom and Dad.

I look over and see Ethan is motioning for me to pull over. We pull onto a dirt road and he stops. He jumps off his bike and unzips his pants. I laugh, knowing the pee dance all too well. He relieves himself and comes to my bike. "Man, I forgot how easy it is to lose yourself on a ride in the country." I can only agree with him. I can see something is bothering him. He keeps looking at me like he wants to say something. "Bry, I'm scared, dude."

I look to make sure he's serious. I have never known him to be scared of shit. "Scared of what, man?"

"Detoxing." Bam, here we go with excuses. I will have a solution to every problem he throws my way. I know he told me when he helped me detox it was the craziest shit he had ever seen.

"I'll be there for you man, just as you were for me. I'm not going to lie to you. It's the hardest thing I ever went through. Just remember that on the flip side, it was the best decision I ever made, without regret."

His silence worries me, but I know he is going through it all in his head. He needs this time. He needs to process the reasons why. He has to do this for himself, for his future.

"You need to promise me, you will keep Ramie away. You and I, that's it. I want it like I did it for you, Bro." That's not hard, and I can do it.

"Of course, dude. This is not shit you want everyone to know. I, of all people, understand that one hundred percent. We can do it at my place. I will be there to see you through it all."

I send a text to Ramie to let her know we are good, and on our way back to town. She texts me back to say she is cooking dinner. Whoa. Two home cooked meals in one day? Damn, I must be doing something right. I let Ethan know she's cooking, and we can stop to get some wine to go with dinner. I think we deserve a little celebrating.

As we approach the front porch, I smell it. There is no way she is cooking what I think she's cooking. I step up my pace and hurry to the kitchen. Low and behold, she damn sure is cooking my favorite food in the world, gumbo. Holy shit balls, she even has potato salad on the stove. I pick her up and spin her around a couple of times and kiss her cheek. "Sweetpea, you keep cooking like that, you'll have me on one knee begging you to marry me." She throws her head back and laughs so hard she snorts. Ethan on the other hand is glaring at me with a look to kill.

"Just because you saved her from that fucktwat, doesn't mean our deal is voided. Hands off my family, remember?"

Now it's my turn to laugh. "I would never cross that line, dickweed, and you know it."

Ramie throws the dish towel down in the sink, "Don't I have a say so in whom I marry? I am of age, and, the last time I checked, that gives me the legal right to do as I please. But, just to get things straight once and for all, Bryson is a dream. A woman's man, built to please. Well, he's just fine as fuck… but I wouldn't have him if he was the last man on Earth!"

Well just fuck my ego! What the hell did I do to piss her off? "Why is that, Ramie? What happen between breakfast and dinner? Before I left, I was your HERO." She gives me this look like I should know why.

"Well for one, your three F club you always brag about, "find them, fuck them, and forget them. Two, you have sworn off love, saying you will never love again. Three, you go through women like I go through perfume, fast and furious, so let's get real here. I want a man to love me. Treat me with respect in and out of the bedroom. I want him to call me twenty times a day to just to hear my voice, and see how my day is going, and to send me flowers just because he thinks I need a smile. He will take me to dinner and a movie, and to meet his friends."

Wow, she dreams big. "Ramie, sweetheart, that's the kind of man you deserve. And you're right, it's not me."

Ethan pipes in about this time with his two cents. "Bryson didn't even have that with Leah. I always wondered why you married her, dude. I don't think you even loved her. I think she was your comfort zone, and you needed that after high school. She was not the love of your life like you thought she was. I believe your soul mate will pop up when your guard is down. That shit is going to slap you in the face so fast you won't know what hit you."

What the fuck is up with these two bitches? "I thought you two were my best friends? You both just went straight for my jugular. With friends like you I don't need any enemies!" Ramie jumps up and comes to hug me.

"I love you, Bryson. I would die for you. I want true love, and I know you're not capable of that. I will just love you like a brother. I know my forever is somewhere out there."

She places a big steaming hot bowl of gumbo and potato salad in front of me, and is instantly forgiven. Where in the hell did she learn how to cook like this? My grandmother was the only one that could cook gumbo that I would eat. I always thought it was because she was Cajun, but Ramie is from Texas and I am pretty sure she doesn't have any Cajun in her.

After two large bowls and a bottle of wine, I don't think I can handle another drop. I notice Ethan is not looking too well. He didn't eat or drink much. I ask him if he's okay. He shakes his head, and says he's going to pack a quick bag so we can be on our way. I help Ramie with the dishes and thank her again for dinner. I promise to take her out to eat one night because my cooking skills really suck.

She gives me a look like I just grew horns, "You are going to be seen in public, at a restaurant, with a female? What will that do for your reputation of, 'I don't take anyone to dinner'?"

I give her the stink eye and pop her with the dish towel "You're my little sister, so that's different. If anyone has anything to say about it they can kiss my country ass."

That gets a full gut laugh out of her. I tell her that Ethan and I are going to be staying at my house, letting her know we need a few days to cram for finals. She buys it, and says she will hold down the fort while we are gone. I lay out all the rules I want her to follow while we are gone. Like, no boys allowed, in the house, locking all doors, and not to answer if Ryan or Noah comes by. She grins, but she knows I'm serious. I let her know I am only a phone call away, and I can be here in ten minutes, tops, if she needs me. We pinky promise, and I give her a hug before leaving.

Ethan and I head straight to my place because Ethan is starting to look rough, and I know what that means. When we get there, I tell Ethan he can take the guest room and get a quick shower. I then make a quick call to my mom and let her know I had a good day, and I miss her. I need to touch base with her, or she will start calling. After I talk to Mom for a few more minutes, Ethan emerges from his room. I let my mom know that Ethan and I will be turning our phones off for a few days so we can cram for finals. She wishes us luck, and we say goodbye.

"Bryson, Bro. I feel fucking sick as a dog. I threw up everything I ate earlier. I think it's starting." Shit, I was hoping to get a shower and prepare things before this started.

"Sleep, dude. You should sleep as much as you can. You know the next step will suck ass." He nods his head and goes to his room. I will give him a little bit before I go check on him. I know this is the easy part. All you want to do is sleep for the first day or so, and when you wake up, the shit starts. I need to make sure we have enough food because he will be starved. All you want to do is eat everything in the house. Damn, I hate that he has to go through this shit. I wouldn't wish this on my worst enemy, much less my best friend.

A little while later, I crack open the door and he's snoring. Everything is good for now, so I quietly shut the door and head for the shower. The water feels amazing but, the thoughts from six months ago come flooding in. I remember being so angry and wanting to just punch anyone and anything around. I remember wanting to make people hurt like I was hurting. Ethan took so much shit from me. I'm really hoping I can do the same for him. I had so much anger towards Leah for what she had done. I blamed her for getting hooked up with that shit. Meth is not something anyone wants to get involved with. I have seen meth tear up so many lives. Now I have to watch my friend go through this. This really is going to suck.

Chapter 7

Jenna

The next couple of weeks go well. I keep up with the cooking and cleaning, and make sure I am in my room before Clay returns home. It all works out well, and no one fights or gets hurt. I continue to give Bryan my list and he brings me the things I need. Morning sickness is getting better, but I know I need to see a doctor soon.

Deciding it's time to google about pregnancy, I grab my iPad, along with my sprite and crackers, and get settled. I read up on pregnancy, and just as I thought, I NEED A DOCTOR NOW!! I really need prenatal vitamins for me and the baby. I typed in the day I know I got pregnant, and it tells me my due date is September thirtieth. That means I am now close to five months pregnant and way behind on everything. Now, I am worried and need to see a doctor. How am I going to see a doctor without anyone finding out? I have to figure something out quick.

The next morning, I knock on Bryan and Caden's doors to let them know breakfast is ready. "Is there any special breakfast foods you like? I can cook just about anything."

Bryan speaks up. "I love pancakes, but I know they take a long time. I would hate to put you through all that trouble." I smile because he is so sweet.

"Bryan, not only do I know how to make them, I make them from scratch. Do you have a favorite kind? I mean, do you like banana or blueberry or strawberry?" His eyes go wide.

"You can make them fruity, too? I really love strawberry." Now I have to laugh at him. He looks like a kid that's just been told he can have chocolate.

"Great, let me put that on the list. How about we get different kinds of fruits, and I can let you both try different ones?" Caden nods his head eagerly.

"I eat anything, so I will try them all! My favorite is banana, but I never ate it in pancakes before." There is just something about this kid that makes me want to do everything to watch him smile.

"Cool, so Bryan you get to pick different fruits and surprise us with your choices." I add fruit to the list and hand it back to Bryan.

Before Bryan gets to his car, I run out to stop him. "Bryan, wait...you said if I needed anything to just ask. This is not easy for me but, do you think I can drop you at work tomorrow? I need to use your car to do a few things in town."

He smiles that sweet smile of his and says, "You got it, rich girl. Just as long as you're there to pick me up after my shift." We discuss the arrangements, and he says he must go before he is late. I run back inside to get the kitchen clean. When I open the door, Louise grabs my hair and drags me to my bedroom. Oh. My. God. *What is wrong with this crazy woman?* I scream for her to let me go, that she is hurting me.

"Shut the hell up, you little slut! I know your type, and I will not have you trying to get my son to have sex with you." What the hell is wrong with her? Is she out of her mind?

"Louise, no. I would never do that. I'm not a slut. I just... I needed him to get more groceries for dinner." Caden comes in and yells for her to get out and leave me alone. She swings back and slaps him across the face. It shocks me, and I grab her arm so she can't hit him again, and she raises her other hand to slap me. I am so happy when I see Bryan grab her arm to stop her.

"Mom, stop it! Don't you dare put another hand on her! Do you hear me?" She turns to glare at him, but lets me go. Caden runs and puts his head in my chest.

"Jenna, I am so sorry I couldn't protect you." I grab his little face and make him look at me.

"Caden, look at me, honey. I'm okay, she didn't hurt me. You stopped her, and you did protect me." I know in his mind he's replaying the last incident that happened with his mother and her pimp before she shot him when he runs off to his room.

I look over to Bryan, and he turns to his mom once more, "If you ever touch one hair of either one of them kids again, I swear to God and all the angels in Heaven that I will march my ass to social services and tell them everything, and I mean everything. You get paid to raise these children and protect them, not abuse them. Do you hear me?"

She stares at him, "Yes, I hear you, and I'm disgusted with you. How can you stand there and turn your back on your own flesh and blood for that little bastard? He will amount to nothing, and that bitch only wants to get in your bed."

My mouth drops open, and I can't believe what I'm hearing. How dare she call Caden and me such names? And she gets paid to keep us here? I step around them in search of Caden, and I find him in his room crying in a corner. I sit beside him and pull his head to my lap, running my fingers through his hair trying to console him. "It's okay, baby boy. I'm fine, I promise."

After a few seconds of silence he speaks up, "Is the baby okay? Did she hurt it?"

I'm speechless. How does he know? "The baby is fine, Caden. She didn't hit me, she only pulled my hair. Can you please tell me how you knew I was pregnant?" He wipes the tears from his face.

"You always hold your baby. My mom used to do it when she was pregnant with my sisters. Her boyfriends would hit her and pull her around by her hair. She always protected her belly." My God this baby breaks my heart. He should never have witnessed these things. What do I say to him? Are there any words? I just hold him close and let him work through his emotions.

When Bryan comes in to check on us, he tells us he is not going into work today. "I just talked to Megan and she is willing to work my shift. I want to take you both somewhere to get you away from here for the day." We both jump up and hug Bryan.

"That sounds great to me. I will get changed and be out in a minute. Caden, you should also get some better clothes on." He frowns, and I ask him what's wrong.

"This is all I have. All my clothes look like this. I will stay here and just go to the woods until you get home." I think that was the last straw for me.

"No, Caden, you will not stay here. You can come in what you have. Bryan, can you take me to my house in Houston?" He says he will take me anywhere I needed or wanted to go. I have a plan. I just need to get to my house for ten minutes.

The clothes Caden has on should have been burned years ago, but I won't let that ruin our day. I style his hair the best way I can, and make a mental note to get him a haircut soon. We all leave without a word to Louise, not that she cares anyway.

We make it to Houston in an hour, and I give Bryan directions to my house. When we pull up Caden is in awe, "Who lives here?"

I laugh and tell him, "This is my home. I was born and raised right here."

He smiles and replies, "I knew you were a rich girl." I tell him to shut up.

"Come on in here. Make yourselves at home. I have to get a few things upstairs, and then I will give you a tour." I open the door and put in the code on the alarm. They both just stand there, looking around like they are in an art gallery.

"Come on, guys. It's just a house." I run up to my room and grab a suit case. I load it up with a few things. Then I go to my father's, office and open the safe. "Sorry, Daddy but you always said this money was available for the things we needed. I promise it's needed, and will be used well. You and Mom would be so proud of me."

When I call downstairs to see if Bryan and Caden would help to get my suitcase down the stairs, they both race up and grab the bag. As we walk though the kitchen, Caden spots the pool out back.

"Holy Shit balls, dude! Look at this pool."

Bryan goes over and takes a look, and shakes his head, "When can we come back for a swim, rich girl?"

Laughing I tell them, "Anytime you guys want. This is all mine when I turn eighteen. I mean, it's mine now, but it will be in my name when I turn eighteen." Their faces turn sad and I wonder what I said, "Why the sad faces?"

They look at each other and back to me, "We don't want to think about you leaving us anytime soon." Awe, how sweet.

"Please, don't make me think about that now, or I will start crying. I promise not to forget you when I leave. You know where I live now, so you can come by or call me anytime."

As we lock up and head to the car, I ask them if they would like to go to the mall. Bryan is ready and willing, but Caden says he has never been to the mall. Bryan and I turn to stare at him, and then look at each other and laugh it off. "You are in for a treat, baby boy. That's all I can say about that." This trip is definitely going to be fun.

When we get inside the mall, I tell Caden that if he sees anything he wants to look at to just let me know and we will go look. We are in front of American Eagle when he stops and stares. "Come on, Caden. Let's go see what they have that you may like." We go in and he starts pulling shirts off the rack and admiring them. We get his size of a few different ones, then move on to jeans and shorts. I get a clerk to take them to the dressing room and we continue to shop. We choose a few more and make our way to try them on. While he is trying them on, I go and get more. Handing them to the clerk, I ask her to ring them up and bag them before he comes out. When he's done he brings them out, and I ask Bryan to take him to Game Stop to show him the games there. I don't want him to see the amount of the clothes. There are just some things kids don't need to know.

After I pry them away from the games, we go into Foot Locker. This kid loses his shit. He is grabbing shoes and telling us how he has seen people at school with them. He tells us he's always dreamed of having shoes like this. Needless to say, we bought him three pairs before walking out. He even begs to wear the last pair to finish shopping. The sales person agrees it would be fine, and took the box to scan. The smile on this kids face is priceless. I wish he could keep that smile forever.

Smelling the aroma coming from the Food Court makes my stomach grumble. "What do you guys think about getting some Chinese? I love it, but for some reason I can't cook it."

Bryan nods but Caden shrugs and replies, "I have never eaten it, but I will eat just about anything." I go ahead and order what I think he will like and, after I put in my order,

Bryan makes his. After we sit and eat, we listen to all the excitement Caden has about being in the mall. He can't stop talking about the games he played and how much fun he had. He also talks about how much fun he and Bryan could have if they had a Playstation or X-box at home. We shop until we can't carry another bag. I sure hope Bryan has a big trunk.

On our way home, Bryan stops off to get my list of groceries. I ask if we could join him, and maybe pick out things we all like for late night snacking. He agrees, and we all go inside. We start off with one buggy, and less than half way through the store, Bryan goes to get another cart. Caden is like a kid in a candy store, but he always asks, "Jenna, do we have enough to buy this?"

"Yes, Caden, I have enough to buy whatever we want here. Now will you please just get things you would like to have at home?" He smiles and nods.

When we are checking out and the cashier gives the total. Caden says softly, "Jenna we can put back the things I chose. I don't really need them. This is too much money."

Bless his little heart, "No we don't have to put anything back. I have the money to pay for all of it."

He looks at me with such confusion, "Are you really rich? I only called you rich girl because your clothes were so pretty and you smell so good."

Bryan and I burst out laughing, "No honey I am not rich, but my dad had a good job and my mom saved a lot. That means we never had to worry about money. They are both gone now, so the money is mine. I promise this is not going to break me." His smile is back and he seems satisfied with the answer. I just hope this all fits in the car with everything we got from the mall.

The closer we get to home, our moods change. No more jokes, smiles or laughter. Bryan tells us to stay put until he goes in to make sure they are in bed. He comes out and lets us know the coast is clear but to watch for broken glass on the floor. I am so happy that we missed that shit.

As we begin unloading the car, Caden takes the bags from my hands. "No ma'am, no lifting for you. Please, let Bryan and me do this. You go inside and put them away."

Awe! "Thank you. That's very nice of you. You're such a gentleman."

Once inside, I pick up the larger pieces of glass and sweep up the rest. This makes no sense. These people need to seek mental help. I ask Bryan and Caden to bring my suit case and the bags from the mall to my bedroom. Once we have things put away, we all go to my room to separate our purchases. When Caden figures out he has five times more clothes than he had chosen, he is speechless. "Jenna this is too much, you must bring some back. No one needs this many clothes. You can get your money back to use for something else."

I pull him in for a hug, "Caden, all my life I've had anything and everything I ever asked for. Now, I want to pay-it-forward and give it to you. When you're older and have money to spare, I would like for you to do the same for someone else, okay?"

He thinks a minute and responds, "Jenna, when I have a good job and money I plan to do so much for kids like me. I want to help kids like you are helping me. I never knew people like you existed. You showed me that nice people will come if you wait and pray long enough. I know God sent you here to help me until my mom and sisters come for me."

I believe he just took my breath away, and I cry. "I think you're right, baby boy. But, I think God sent me here because he knew I needed you."

Bryan coughs and says, "Hey, what about me? Remember, I am the one with the car." We all laugh and go into a group hug. I give Bryan the gifts I snuck in when he was at Game Stop. It's only a few shirts, shorts, and cologne. He's in shock, and scolds me for spending my money on him. I tell him if he doesn't stop I will never allow him to do anything for me again. This seems to work, and he thanks me. He hugs my neck once more, and then leaves the room.

After a quick shower and having brushed my teeth, I lay in my bed and replay the entire day in my head. As I rub my belly, I tell my baby, "I'm going to buy you everything, and I will love and cherish you like my mom loved me. People like Clay and Louise will never have a chance to hurt you, EVER!"

Bryan walks in and his eyes lock on my hands, "Jen are you..?" His eyes meet mine, and the tears start to roll down my face.

"Yes, but please, please, don't say anything. The only people that know are my best friend Angel, Caden, and well, now you." He closes the distance between us and takes my head to his chest.

"Don't cry, Jen. Your secret is safe with me. What I want to know is how far along are you? Why haven't you been to any doctor's appointments like most pregnant women?" I pull away from him and sit back on my bed.

"That's why I asked you if I could use your car tomorrow. I made an appointment for 9:00 am, but it's in Houston. If you would rather not, I can call Angel to come get me."

He glares at me with a sad smile, "I told you I would help you in any way possible. Using my car to see a doctor is definitely okay. If you can't be there to get me, I can get someone to bring me home. I can also wait in town until you get there." I thank him and he asks me where the father is. I wish I had that answer. I explain a little about it being a one night stand, and how he doesn't answer my calls. We talk for a few minutes and he lets me know, once again, that he is here if I need anything.

Chapter 8

I get out the shower, get dressed and go to the kitchen for a big bowl of ice cream before I start my paper for finals. I prefer to get this paper done while all is calm with Ethan. Damn, I love ice cream I could live on this shit. I pick up my backpack, and just as I am getting settled, my phone buzzes on the counter.

*Are you busy?

**Who is this?

*Leah

**Yeah I'm very busy

*Don't be like this Bry

**Don't call me that and I have some work to do. Deuces

The phone starts ringing and I ignore it. It rings again and again, and I keep hitting ignore.

After the seventh time I pick up the phone. "What Leah? What the fuck do you want?"

I hear her breath catch, "Please don't do this, Bry. I have told you over and over how sorry I am. I need you in my life. I can't stand being away from you."

What the fuck is this bitch up to now? We haven't talked in over a year, so why now? "Leah I don't have time for your shit. I have a paper I need to work on. I also have a woman on her way to take care of my bedroom needs. So just tell me why you had to talk to me?" I don't have time for this bitch.

"Why do you do this to me? I still love you and need you. I know you still love me, too."

I burst out laughing, "What kind of fucking drugs are you on, woman? I don't love you and the more I think about it, the more I think I never did love you. So, if you're done, I really need to go."

Silence. Crying. Oh boy, here we go. Does she think this will get me back? Well, she can think again. She wasn't crying when I caught her fucking Noah. She had her chance to try to make it right. She chose to let me know she loved him. That's the day my heart left my chest with no plans of returning, and that's just the way I want it.

"Can I ask you for a favor?" Sure. Like I am the one to ask for a favor.

"What, Leah?" I wish she would do me a favor and hang up.

"I'm in trouble, Bry. I need to borrow some money." Now if that doesn't just take the cake. This bitch got a settlement in court and half the shit I bought while we were married. Now she has the audacity to ask me to borrow money.

"What fucking tree did you fall out of Leah? I don't care what kind of trouble you're in. You will never get a dime more out of me as long as I live." I hang up the phone and laugh at her stupidity. How could she even think I would give her money?

I hear a cry from the room and run to see what's up. When I get to the door I hear Ethan call my name. "I'm here bro, right here. What do you need?"

"I'm sick man. I can't do this. Please, I can't handle it. I'm not strong like you. Call someone, get me some stuff." Dammit, I was hoping he would just sleep.

"You can Ethan, you are strong. Hell, man, you're the strongest person I've ever known. Just rest, dude. You will feel better in the morning."

He shakes his head, "I'm hungry, but my stomach is sick. Please, dude, you need to help me."

I run to the kitchen and get some crackers and a coke. I come back and get him to try some to see if it helps. He eats the whole pack and drinks the coke. "Lay back and rest, bro. You need to sleep, just like when you have the flu. As long as you sleep, you don't feel sick. He nods his head and lies back down. I pace his room until I hear him snore, and then I make sure he is okay before I go back to my paper.

About four hours later without a sound from him, I get worried. I go to check on him and he's still out. I get my pillow and a blanket, and hit the couch and get comfy. I skim through the channels on the television and find nothing interesting, so I lay there and think about the call from Leah. I can't believe she had the nerve to call me for money. I can't wait to tell that one to Ethan. He will get a good laugh out of it.

When I wake up, it's 10:00 a.m. and I run to Ethan's room only to find him still sleeping. I take a deep breath and go to make coffee, wishing Ramie was here to make us a good ass breakfast. Well, it looks like cereal is the only thing on the menu, so I fix me a big bowl and dig in. When I stand to go put the bowl in the sink, I hear glass breaking in the bedroom. I haul ass to the room, and Ethan has shattered the mirror. "It's cool, dude I hated that mirror anyway." He looks at me with a blank stare like he is ready to rip my head off. "Ethan? You ok, bro?"

"No, I'm not ok. I'm hungry and the smell of coffee is making me sick."

Here it comes, anger and hate. Lord, help me. This is the part I have been dreading. "No problem bro, I will go throw it out and get you some breakfast. Any requests? You know my cooking sucks, so you can choose toast or cereal."

"Toast and a coke," is his reply so I go to get that for him. When I return he is out again. I smile and go back to the kitchen for my coffee. Hours go by without a sound. I go do my work out and get a quick shower. I check in on him again, and he's still out. I get a few other things finished around the house to try and keep myself busy.

Later that evening, I order Chinese from down the street, and have it delivered. Watching out of the window because I don't want them to ring the doorbell and wake Ethan, I meet the delivery boy on the porch when he finally arrives. Damn, I love Chinese. I wonder if I could find me a little Chinese woman to cook for me. I laugh at my own joke. I don't want any woman around me longer than two hours. I eat half of what I ordered, and put the rest up for when Ethan wakes up.

Around 9:00 p.m. I start to worry because Ethan hasn't eaten in a long time. I wonder if I should wake him to eat? I fight myself on what to do, so I decide to call Josh, my sponsor for Narcotics Anonymous. He tells me it's normal for him to sleep up to three days. I thank him, and decide to do my laundry since I am not one to be inside all day. I will lose my mind if I don't keep busy. I sure hope he sleeps through the night.

At 7:00 a.m., I walk into the kitchen and hear talking in Ethan's room. I go to see who he's talking to, but when I get to his room Ethan is alone and still asleep. I stand there for a while, and he starts talking again.

"Leah, I mean it. Get away from me. I am not going to fuck you! You were my best friend's wife." I freeze, not understanding what he means. I wait to see if he says more, which he doesn't. I make the decision to wake him up, so he can explain.

I go get him a Coke from the fridge, and put it beside his bed. "Ethan, bro. Wake up and drink something. Here, I got you a cold Coke." He sits up, and drinks half in one swallow. He puts it down and just looks at me, knowing something is wrong.

"Ethan, I have a question for you, and I need you to be completely honest with me." He looks confused and nods his head. "Did you ever have sex with Leah?"

He squints his eyes and his lips go hard, "Are you fucking crazy, Bryson? What kind of a fucking friend do you think I am? Have we ever hit on each other's girls?"

I need to change the way that came out. "That didn't come out right, bro. Let me try it again. When I came in to check on you, you said something in your sleep, and I just need you to clear it up for me."

Now, the look he gives me is kind of scary. "What did I say Bryson that has you asking such stupid shit?"

I guess the best thing to do is come clean. "You were telling Leah you wouldn't have sex with her because she was my wife." He puts his head down, and I don't like the feeling I am getting in my stomach.

"Bry, I was at a party at Noah's one night, and Leah was screwing everyone she could get in the bed. I didn't understand what was going on until later when she tried to get me to go with her. Dude, she wanted me to pay her for sex. She needed a fix and didn't have the money. I never would have slept with Leah for the simple fact she was yours. Knowing she was selling herself made the situation even worse. I thought of telling you about it many times, but I knew it would fuck with your head and you would try to blame yourself."

I can't believe what he's telling me. "Are you telling me Leah is on meth, too, and she is selling her body to get meth to feed her addiction?" He nods his head again, and I think I am going to lose my shit. Did she turn to that shit because I left her? No, I will not take that blame. She was cheating on me. This is not my fault. "I won't take that blame Ethan. It is not my blame to take. She chose him and he got her hooked on that shit, not me."

Ethan lifts his head and smiles, "I'm so glad you see it that way. I am sorry I never told you, but I was scared you would try to turn it on yourself." I shake my head and tell him about her calling me for money yesterday. That pissed him off. The anger phase has kicked in. He starts to tremble and shake and I see fire in his eyes. I try to calm him and laugh about her calling me. It doesn't stop his anger. I tell him to chill, and ask him if he wants some food. That seems to work and we go to the kitchen for him to eat. Damn, now I know Leah is a trigger for him.

Ethan is shoveling food into his mouth like we shovel horse shit on the ranch. I tell him to slow down and that the food is not going anywhere. Giving me the mean eye, he goes back to eating. When he finally finishes eating, he goes to take a shower and comes out looking so much better.

"How are you feeling, bro?"

"I need to take a nap."

"Sure, dude. Go ahead a take a nap. I have some papers I need to finish before finials anyway." I reply.

After Ethan heads back to his room, I send a quick text to Ramie.

- Hey, Sweetpea. How's it going there?

- It's all good, Sexy. Are you getting any smarter? Lol

- Haha smartass.

- Sorry I couldn't help it.

- I bet you couldn't. It's all cool here.

- Do you want me to come over with some good home cooking?

- Nah we're good I got Chinese delivered.

- Fine. You really don't know what to do with a good woman do you?

- Sweetpea, are you trying to ruffle my feathers? You know I can handle any woman at any time. I just choose not to. GTG call if you need me.

- Sure thing, Cowboy.

I check in on Ethan and he's out again. Man this seems too easy. I just worry this is the calm before the storm.

Later that afternoon, Mom calls and I am bored, so I decide to answer. She asks a few questions on how the cramming is coming along, and if I am eating well. You know, the whole "mother thing". We talk about Dad and the ranch, and how much work he has in his business. I know he can't wait for me to finish so I can take some of the load off of him. She also tells me about a new foster girl that will be placed in their home. Mom said she's pregnant and that makes me nervous. Mom always gets her hopes up that one of these girls will not want their baby, and she will be able to adopt it.

My mom was only able to have me, and the doctors told her I was a miracle. She was blessed to have me with the way her tubes were so messed up. She has always wanted a girl. Taking in these pregnant girls and fostering them is the closest she has come to having her girl. I make her promise me she will not get her hopes up again. We talk a bit more before I let her know I have to get back to my studying.

After hanging up, I think about how some low-life could let their pregnant girlfriend go into foster care. Does he know she is carrying his child? Men that fuck like men should be man enough to act like men when it comes to their children. People like that need a good ass whipping. I shake my head and go to work out.

In the middle of the night, I hear a loud noise coming from the hall. I run to Ethan's room and find what I have been dreading. There is angry Ethan, shaking, trembling, and gritting his teeth. I move slowly towards him and his breathing gets heavier. I put my hands out as a calming signal, but that doesn't seem to work, so I stop. "Ethan, bro. You need to calm down, and we can talk about what's got you upset." He slows down his breathing but he's still angry. "What's got you pissed, dude? Talk to me so I know."

Ethan gives me a look that says he could kill me, so I wait for him to speak. "You, Bryson, you are my problem. You think you are better than me. You think you're all that and you can do whatever you want with whomever you wish. Well, fuck you. You are no better than the rest of us."

Whoa, where the hell did that come from? I wait because I have a feeling he is not done with me yet. I am not going to defend myself. I know he needs to get this out. I wait and wait until I think he's done, and then he stands and walks closer to me.

"You think I can't have the women you've had? You think you're the only one that can walk away from drugs and never turn back? You think you're the only one that can perform on a football field? Well, I'm here to tell, you I can do it too, and, I don't need your damn help!"

"No, Ethan, I don't think any of that. I know I go through withdraws at times. You don't think I know it would be easier to take a hit and go to La-La Land than to deal with some of the shit I deal with, bro? And, as far as being a big shot on the field? You were better than I could even dream about being. *You* decided to let that shit take over your life. If it wasn't for my ex-wife deciding to cheat on me, I wouldn't even know what another woman felt like. I never wanted another woman as long as I had her. She was my one and only for six years, man."

Ethan turns and walks back to the bed and thinks for a while. I wait for more to come, but it doesn't. He just sits there shaking. I walk out and send a text to Josh in hope of guidance.

- Hey, Josh you got a minute?

- Sure, man. What's up?

- I think we hit the anger stage.

- Ah, now the fun begins.

- He's angry at me, and that sucks.

- He's angry at the world, Bryson, but you're the only one there he can take it out on. Is he getting physical?

- No, it's like he is trying to hurt me with words.

- If you can take it, let him get it out. I believe y'alls friendship can handle it. Just remember he will go through the sorrow stage as well. You doing great, Buddy. I am really proud of you.

- Thanks, man. I needed to know that.

- No problem. Let me know if I can help.

I bring him a big bowl of ice cream in hopes of getting him to calm down. He takes the bowl and eats like he's starving. Man either I can't remember this part, or maybe everyone deals with it in different ways. We talk a while and he seems to have calmed. "How are you feeling, Bro?"

"My body aches and I feel sick. I also feel bad about what I said to you, Bry. You know I love you like a brother and I would never hurt you. I am really sorry."

"I know, dude. I won't let that shit get to me. I understand what you're going through. Our friendship goes deeper than that."

I see Ethan's body has relaxed, but he looks tired again. "I have some shit I need to get done. Go get you some sleep. Give a shout if you need me."

"Thanks, Bry." As I walk out I hear him say, "I'm so lucky to have a friend like you, Bry. I don't know what I would do if you gave up on me."

I give him my half smile, "Same here man and I am the lucky one. True friends like you are few and far between."

Chapter 9

Jenna

I am up before anyone else this morning, so I sneak into Caden's room and tell him to get ready quietly, and make sure he puts on some of his new clothes. I then go back to my room, and wait for Clay to leave. Once he leaves the house, I hurry to make banana pancakes. After setting them on the table, I watch as Bryan and Caden devour them. I send Caden to brush his teeth and hair while I get the kitchen cleaned.

When we reach the car Bryan says, "Hey, rich girl," I turn and he tosses me the keys. I guess this means I'm driving us. This just adds to my excitement. My emotions are all over: happy, nervous, sad and a little worried.

After dropping Bryan off at work, and promising him to be on time to pick him up, Caden and I are Houston bound.

I made the appointment with the OB/GYN that delivered me and saw me for my first yearly checkups. I had always promised Mom I would tell her before I decided to have sex so we could discuss it and get me a doctor's appointment to get protection. Dr. Lacy has a granddaughter my age, and we were on the cheer squad together. I guess you could say Dr.Lacy is a family friend. When I spoke to her yesterday, she insisted I came today. That made me very nervous. I just pray everything is okay.

Mom would be so supportive, but I know she would also have a broken heart. I wish I could have told her.

Caden sees my expression and reaches over to give my hand a squeeze, "Why are you so sad, Jenna? Did I do something wrong?"

His sad face is heart shattering, "No, honey. You did nothing wrong. Why would you even think that?"

He shrugs his shoulders and says, "Your face went sad, so I just figured I did something to make you sad. When my mom was sad, she always said it was me who made her sad."

"Oh, baby boy. I was just thinking of my mom. I never got to tell her I was going to have a baby, and I was wondering how she would have felt about it. In a way, I know she would have supported me and loved my baby, but I also know it would have broken her heart. I never liked seeing my mom sad."

He gives my hand a tight squeeze and says, "I don't like seeing you sad either, Jenna. If you tell me how to make you happy, I will try so hard to do it."

I smile the biggest smile and watch his face light up. "Seeing you happy and smiling makes me smile." We drive a while, singing and laughing and making faces at other drivers.

Caden turns the radio down and says "Jenna, I'm happy you're having a baby. I really miss my little sisters. I will help you with it. I know how to change diapers, give baths, and prepare bottles. Babies are hard work, but when they smile at you, it's like they are saying 'thank you'."

I don't have the heart to tell him I won't be there with him when I have this baby. So instead, I tell him "I bet you were a great big brother." He smiles sobig and you can tell he's remembering his own sisters.

Before long we are pulling into a parking space at Dr. Lacy's office, and we spot Angel pacing at the front door. I shake my head as we make our way to her.

"Bitch, it's about time you got here. I have been going insane worrying that you were not coming or you were in a wreck. I even thought those crazy people locked you up and wouldn't let you come." Caden and I just laugh at how fast she gets that all out. My BFF is the worry wart and sometimes thinks she is my mother.

I introduce Angel to Caden as we walk in, and she automatically dives in with her mountain of questions, like always. Caden answers each and every one, while I go check in. While we sit and wait to be called back, Angel starts drilling me on how things are going in the home. I decide against telling her all the bad things. I let her know that I get to cook. and shop. I tell her that Caden and Bryan keep me from being depressed. Caden keeps up with our conversation and agrees with what I say. I think she buys it. Well, I pray she does.

I change the subject to Angel's job, and ask how it is working out. Her face lights up, and now her mouth is going full speed. Seems she has made new friends. This makes me a little sad. I can't be mad, I have made new friends, too. Not that they could replace her, but they are definitely good friends.

The nurse calls my name and we all stand up. I turn and look at them both. Do I want them in there with me? Caden speaks up "I will wait here if I want me to, Jenna. If they do a thing that shows the baby, I want to see it, please."

I turn to the nurse and ask "Are they are allowed in?" She nods and waves us in. After all the vitals and weight are taken she leads us to a room. Now my nerves are really kicking in.

Our wait is not long before Dr. Lacy comes in, "Nice to see you Jenna and Angel. I don't think I ever met this handsome young man?" I introduce her to Caden and he shakes her hand. He lets her know he is my foster brother. She ask if I am comfortable talking in front of them. I let her know that it's fine.

After all the questions are answered and dates are put in Dr. Lacy says "Jenna, I would like to do an ultrasound today, just to make sure everything looks okay. I want to make sure all is well with the baby's growth."

"Sure Dr. Lacy, whatever you think is best." She pulls my pants below my belly and applies some really cold gel. She begins to move a wand over my stomach, and all of a sudden I hear it, OH MY GOD! it's my baby's heartbeat! She points and shows me the heart beating, "There's your little one, Jenna. The heartbeat is strong and looks like it's right on track. It's measurements are spot on with the growth chart. I think it's safe to say you are doing well. Keep it up and make sure you drink a lot of water. The heat can get you when you least expect it."

I can make out that it's a baby. Tears flow like rain and I am smiling so big my jaw hurts. Caden and Angel both ask at the same time "What is it, doc?"

"Well it looks like...well it looks like he/she is being bashful. Let me see if I can get it to move and maybe open up the legs so we can see." She moves the wand around and pushes my stomach in different spots, but the baby refuses to move.

"Well, it looks like we will have to wait until next month to see. I'm really sorry, Caden, but hopefully on the next visit it will open up and let us see."

Of course they both frown and I have to laugh at them, "Come on guys don't be sad, it gives us something to look forward to, right? We got to see the heartbeat and we know it's okay. I do believe that's worth celebrating over lunch at Joe's Crab Shack, right?" I know that is Angel's favorite restaurant, so I will get no argument from her.

After lunch we say our goodbyes to Angel, and head back to "Smallville". There are a few things I need to pick up before we pick up Bryan, so I pull into Wal-Mart, in hopes of completing my to-do-list. First thing, is to get Caden's haircut. We sign in and ask how long before someone can take him. The lady says she can take him now.

Caden turns to me in shock, "I am getting my hair cut? Louise just shaves it. I have never been anywhere to have my hair cut."

I laugh and tell him, "Well today we let a professional cut it. Is there anything special you want?" He thinks a minute.

"Can I have it cut so I can spike it? All the boys in school spike their hair.

"You can have what you want, that's what we're here for." I tell the stylist to give him what he wants. He smiles my favorite toothy smile I love so much.

After Caden's hair is done we set out to get our shopping done. We hurry around the store to get everything on my mental list so we can make it to pick up Bryan on time. Fortunately we make it with little time to spare. When we go in to let him know we are there, Bryan waves at us from the manager's booth. He lets us know he will clock out and be right with us. Caden is staring at the candy display, so I walk over and grab me a Hershey's bar, and I ask him if he see's anything he would like. He goes for a Kit Kat and puts it back to grabs a Butterfinger. I go behind him and snatch up a couple of Kit Kats and put them on the counter. By the time we have paid and make our way back to the Manager's booth, Bryan tells the night manager coming on goodbye, and we leave.

When we are home, Bryan and Caden unload the car and take everything into my room. Bryan gives me crazy looks when he sees everything I bought, but he never asked a single question. I change quickly and hurry to the kitchen to start dinner. Of course, when I get there the old hag is at the table, like normal. I roll my eyes and begin my food prep. Caden has asked for fried chicken and macaroni and cheese. I'm also adding rice dressing and homemade biscuits to finish off the meal.

I notice Caden has left the house to go out and play with Chase next door, so I go in search of Bryan. I find him in the living room. "Bryan can I get you to help me with something in my room?"

"Sure, I'll be there in a minute."

Once we are there I tell him. "The television is for Caden's room, and I have my Playstation in the suitcase. I was hoping you would set it all up in his room while he's not here? I really would like to surprise him with it."

Bryan's eyes go wide, "Are you serious? You bought the kid his own television? And you're giving him your own personal playstation?"

I giggle and answer, "Yes, why is that so unbelievable? Kids his age should already have these things. Didn't you see him in the Game Stop with all those games? I want to see that smile on his face every day that I have left here."

He shakes his head and grabs the box, "Okay, Rich Girl whatever you want, but this sucks. I don't even have my own T.V." Omg I never realized he didn't have a T.V. in his room. I guess I never knew just how fortunate I was growing up with the parents I had. I really took my family for granted.

I am finishing up in the kitchen when I see Caden come through the front door. I call him in the kitchen to keep him from his room so Bryan can finish up. "Will you set the table for me please, Caden?" That should buy me a few minutes.

"Sure Jen. Are you eating with us tonight?" I wish I could but I have to eat in my room, out of sight of the pervert.

"No honey, I'm going to go to my room to eat, so just set four." He frowns but does as he's told.

Bryan comes in and gives me the thumbs up. When Caden is done, I ask him if he could follow me. I walk into his room and wait for him to notice.

"WHAT THE... how? Where? Jenna, what is this?"

Bryan and I just laugh, "It's yours, baby boy. All yours." He starts crying and puts his arms around me and cries until the tears stop flowing.

"Jenna, I love you so much. You are better to me than my own mom. No one has ever given me anything. My mom always promised one day I could have a game like this, but she never had the money. You can play with me anytime you want."

Bryan pipes in and says he's ready to challenge him at any game he chooses. When Caden realizes he has a library of games, he really freaks out. All I can do is smile as the tears run down my face. I can't ever remember being this happy for someone else. I am walking out of Caden's room when the door slams and I come face to face with the devil himself, Clay.

"Well, well. What do we have here?" I freeze and I can't get a word to form in my throat. Bryan walks out and puts his arm around my waist and introduces me as his friend. Why didn't I think of that? "Well, you are too sexy and smell too good to be with a looser like my son. If you ever want a real man come look me up." He walks off laughing and I see the bottle fly at his head. Louise starts screaming for me to get to my room and not come out. I don't understand what's going on. Bryan pulls me to my room and tells me to stay put until he comes for me.

The yelling continues, I become so worried about Bryan and Caden. I hear Bryan's voice raise and telling his dad to get to his bedroom now, or he will call the police. I hear the door slam across the hall in hopes he is going to pass out. I stayed put for what seemed like hours but I know it was only few minutes before Bryan comes in.

"Jenna, I need you to drive me to the ER please. I look down and see his hand is cut open.

"What happened to your hand, Bryan?" I grab a towel off my dresser.

"It's really best you don't know the story." I grab my purse and a clean towel. Caden is waiting by the door for me. He takes my hand in his as we walk to the car.

Once we are on the road, Caden asks me if Clay hurt me. I let him know I was in my room during the fighting, and Bryan is the one that took it all this time. "Bryan, would you please tell me what happened back there?"

He turns his head towards me and says, "I punched him after Mom hit him with the bottle. Then, I had him by the throat and told him if he spoke to you like that again, I would kill him. He grabbed what was left of the bottle and stabbed my hand to get it off his throat. "Holy shit, I knew he was a creep but to stab your own son? Who the hell does that?

At the ER, we fill out the paperwork, and are told to have a seat in the blue chairs. They call Bryan back within five minutes . We all stand up, but the nurse tells us only one person is allowed in. I let them go and tell them I will wait out here. I am not sure how I will react to the shots. I am not very good with needles.

About a half hour had passed when I see Kathie walk in. I'm pretty sure she sees the shock on my face. She comes and sits next to me, and begins to rip the heart out of my chest.

"Jenna I need you to know why I am here. I have all your belongings in my car. Louise has asked that you be placed elsewhere. She has also requested that you have no contact with the family. This means Caden as well." I don't understand.

"Why, Kathie? I did nothing wrong. I swear."

"We can talk about this in the car, Jenna. We must go now."

"I have to bring Bryan the keys so they can return home." She is very hesitant but allows me to go. The nurse buzzes me in and I go to the room.

Bryan and Caden are sitting on the table waiting while the nurse is cleaning his cut. I get weak in the knees and my stomach starts to do flips. When I go to speak my voice cracks and Bryan immediately asks what's wrong. The tears start to pour as I speak, "Kathie is here to take me to another home. She says I have to go now. I am not to contact you or your family again." They jump off the table and come to me. Bryan is angry and slinging vulgar language.

Caden holds on to me and cries, "Please, Jenna. Please don't leave me. Everyone I love leaves me. Please stay with me. You are my new mom, Jenna, please I need you. I can't live without you. Please, I am begging. I want to go with you. Please, don't leave me behind, Jenna. I trusted you. I love you, please don't leave me behind." I fall to my knees and hold him to my chest.

"I wish I could control this, baby boy. I don't want to leave you, but I need you to be strong okay? Please be strong and stay safe for me please. Bryan, please help. I have to go before she comes back here." Bryan pulls him from me and holds him trying to calm him. I can't take this anymore. I am going to lose my mind. Needing to leave, I turn and run out to the front. Kathie catches up to me and follows me out.

When we reach her car I break down. I have to let her know now, I can't take this stress. "Kathie, I'm pregnant."

She turns to me and the words that come from her mouth are unbelievable, "From what Louise tells me about you, I am not shocked at all."

Did this bitch really just say this shit? Does she believe that drunk? I am ready to spill my guts on what goes on in that house when I remember Caden's words. "Better? This is better. The others are a lot worse." I keep my mouth shut about the home, but I do let her know the baby was conceived the one and only time I had ever, EVER, had sex and it was before my parents died.

She pulls out her phone as I stare out the window and cry. I cry for Caden. I was going to show him all the happiness I could before I left. I was going to bring him to see his sisters. I was going to get him a cell phone. I was going to take him swimming at the beach. Now, all that is gone. WHY GOD, WHY? What did I do so wrong that you punished this kid? He's just an innocent child for Christ sakes. He needs me, and I need him.

Kathie completes her call, and I ask, "Where I am going now, Kathie? I really would prefer a home without other foster kids if possible."

"I was just on the phone with Kristi. She is a foster parent who only takes in pregnant girls. She is really sweet, and will help teach you a lot of things you will need to know. Kristi and John are waiting on you, and they have no other children in the home at this time."

Thank God! I sure hope John's normal. My mind wonders back to Caden. I am so glad I gave him his t.v. and Playstation. At least he will have something to do besides hide in the woods. I wish he was coming with me. Kathie made it clear that he couldn't. I must stay away and not contact them. I wonder what that old hag told Kathie. I can't explain the anger and sadness I am feeling right now. I just hope that one day karma slaps that old bitch in the face. She doesn't deserve to have Caden or Bryan.

Passing through Houston only makes me want home. This reminds me that I have to text Angel and let her know I have moved again. I will not be able to tell her anything about what happened, because she will go off on all these people and not care. If it wasn't for Caden, I would let her, but I have to protect him.

Chapter 10

Jenna

After what seems like forever, we have arrived at a beautiful ranch. The house is beautiful and big. I see horses, cows, and dogs. I sure hope they have ranch hands because I am not a cowgirl.

A beautiful woman with long, blonde hair meets us at the car. She hugs Kathie and comes around to introduce herself to me, "Hi, you must be Jenna? I'm Kristi Alexander, and I am so happy to have you stay with us."

Wow, what a change. I sure hope it stays that way after Kathie leaves. "Hello, Kristi. Jenna Kingsley. It's so nice to meet you. Thank you for having me." She gives me a hug and it feels so nice, almost like Mom's hugs. My heart melts. I hear a man's voice come from the garage and turn to see who it is. A very handsome tall, well-built, and dark haired man walking up with his hand out.

"You must be Jenna? I'm John Alexander. It's so nice to meet you." I take his hand and give it shake.

"Yes, I'm Jenna, and it's so nice to meet you too, John." Well, at least I didn't have to wait a month to meet him.

I hope this is the last time I have to move before going home. Kathie and I go to unload my things, but John and Kristi step up and take the bags. "There will be no lifting for you, young lady." I guess that means she has told them about the baby. Well, at least I don't have to hide it anymore. Kathie hugs me and says her goodbyes and she's gone. The three of us walk into the house and they show me up to my room. I swear their staircase is longer than ours. The house is welcoming. It feels like a real home.

The house is so gorgeous and clean. My room looks like something from a magazine. I have my own bathroom with locks on all the doors.

"John and I will be in the kitchen when you're ready for dinner. You can come meet us there." Wow, I finally get to eat with other humans.

"I will just clean up a bit and be right down, Kristi. Thank you both again for having me." They smile and let me know they are very happy to have me.

I hurry and grab a change of clothes and wash up for dinner. When I get to the kitchen, I witness them in an embrace with big smiles on their faces. This brings back so many memories of Mom and Dad. Even after so many years together they were still in love like they were when they got married. I pray that I can have that. I think my chances of finding someone to love me and a baby that don't belong to them are slim to none. I go to turn away, and Kristi calls my name, "Jenna, honey. Is everything okay? I hope we didn't offend you?"

I smile and tell them, "Oh, no. Not at all, my Mom and Dad were the same way. It just made me think of them." They wave for me to join them and they give me a hug. God, I feel at home here.

I try to help Kristi set the table, but she wouldn't hear of it. We all sit down to eat and John leads us in saying Grace. He includes me in the prayer asking God to watch over me and my unborn child. I have tears in my eyes when he is done, and I thank him. As we eat and talk, they ask a few questions that were pretty easy to answer. We got along well. After dinner, I bring my plate to the kitchen and start to load the dishwasher, Kristi stops me.

"I cannot let you do my job. Please, relax Jenna. We just want you stress free."

"Kristi, I can't just sit here and not do anything. I am used to helping my mom in the kitchen. I have a few secret recipes I can share with you, too. I can prepare them for y'all if you could stand for me to use your kitchen."

She laughs and says, "You can have it anytime you want, but please don't feel obligated. I love to cook, and besides, that's the only reason John married me was because he loved my cooking."

Just like my dad. This is so weird. "Funny you say that. My mom said my dad married her because she was the best cook around." We have a good laugh. I excuse myself to go unpack and take a shower without having to worry about anyone walking in on me. I sure hope things work out for me here. I really like Kristi and John.

My mind is on Caden. He was so destroyed when I left him. I pray that he doesn't blame me. I never wanted to leave him. I was even thinking of ways we could see each after I turned eighteen. I can't believe I can't see or talk to him again. I can't hold back my tears. I slide down the wall of the shower and cry. *Please, God, take care of him. He has nothing and no one but you. Keep him safe and healthy until I can see him again.*

Once I'm done with my shower, I turn on the radio and send a text to Angel. I let her know where I am and how awesome this place is. She is happy to hear it, but she is busy at work and will call me later. I miss my friend. I wish we could see each other more. I hear a soft knock on the door. Kristi asks if she can come in. I open the door and invite her in.

"Jenna I wanted you to know I am here for you if you need anything, even if it's just to talk. I won't judge you. I know every girl needs someone to talk to. I'm not your mom, nor would I ever try to take her place, but I am a mother who understands."

Pinch, me I think I'm dreaming. I swear my mother has been placed into this woman's body. She is just too good to be true. "Thank you Kristi, I really appreciate everything. Yes, I would love to have someone to talk to. I have a close friend back home, but since the accident I have only been able to see her once." She gives me this bright understanding smile.

"Well, we will see what we can do about that. You do have your license right?" I nod my head then my manners kick in.

"Yes, ma'am, I do, and I am a very good driver. I have my own car but because of legal reasons I had to leave it home." She gives my arm a rub.

"What about your doctor's appointments? Where are they?" I wonder if she will want to come with me or not?

"I just saw her yesterday. Dr. Lacy was the OB that delivered me. She was also a family friend, so I thought it best to see someone who would care. She said everything is fine and we did an ultrasound. Would you like to see the pictures?"

Her eyes light up, "Yes, I would love to! I am so happy you decided to go to her. I am sure your mom would have loved that idea as well." I really think my mom is speaking through this woman. God, she says all the right things.

"Yes, I think she would, too. Here are the pictures. She said next month we should know the sex. I am getting really excited. Not that it really matters. I don't care what it is, I will love it forever."

She looks at me with confusion in her eyes. "You're going to keep the baby?" What the hell does she mean by that?

"Of course I am going to keep my baby. This baby is all I have in this world. I have no living relatives. This baby will be my world."

She apologizes, "Oh, Jenna. I am so sorry, I didn't mean it that way. The way Kathie was talking gave me the feeling you were not keeping it." Kathie can kiss my white ass if she thinks I am giving up my baby.

"What would make her think that? I just told her on the way over here that I was pregnant. I never insinuated I was giving it away. I'm not going to lie to you. I will give you the story later when I'm not so tired. The home I just left is not fit to raise animals. I don't know what they told Kathie to make her pull me from there. I am not trash. Excuse my language, but I am not a slut either. I made one mistake and got pregnant. I know who the father is. I have tried to contact him but he never returns my calls. I'm really a good girl with good morals. I just made a huge mistake I can't take back." She pulls me in for a hug and rubs my hair. I cry and she tells me she believes me. We will have that talk later but, for now, I need some rest. She tells me her bedroom is located downstairs. She also stresses that if I need anything, not to hesitate to wake her.

Everything smells so fresh and clean here, just like home. I had a few dreams that broke my sleep during the night. Other than that, I slept well for the most part. I go into the bathroom and relieve my bladder. I brush my teeth and hair and dress for the day. When I get down to the kitchen breakfast is being put on the table. I smile and say, "Good morning." They both turn and return the greeting with beautiful smiles. I ask if I can help and Kristi assures me everything is complete. We all sit down, say grace, and serve our plates.

I reach for my glass and I am blown away. Coffee milk awaits me. I take a deep breath and ask, "Kristi how did you know?"

She gives me her little half smile, "My Bryson loves coffee milk. I took a chance that you would too." I smile and tell her it was the one thing Mom always had ready for me before school. We eat and I ask about her children. She tells me she only has a son. Bryson is in college at LSU in Louisiana. She says how proud she is of him but wishes he would come home more. She goes on to explain he plays football, and he had also gone through a bad divorce last year. She says that took away a lot of their family time. I tell her I'm sorry and hope things get better.

After breakfast dishes are done, Kristi says she has nothing planned for the day, and we can do whatever I want. I hope she is serious about whatever I want. "If you don't mind I would like to stay here and maybe we could talk and get to know each other."

"I would love that, Jenna, and maybe later we can go for a swim." That sounds amazing to me. She leads me to the living room and we sit. She tells me all about how she and John got together and fell in love.

We talk a bit about her miscarriages. Going through five miscarriages seems like the hardest thing on earth to me. I know what one did to my mother. I cannot imagine five. She says two were before Bryson and 3 after him and that's when she gave up. She accepted that she would only have one child. That's when she decided to help teenage girls who were pregnant and in foster care. She makes me feel so loved and special. I think I will be okay here until my birthday. It's only a couple more months away.

I want to ask her help with Caden, but I am so afraid to put him in any danger. After about three hours, she asked if I would like to go for a dip in the pool. Missing my pool at home, I immediately agree. We both go to our rooms to get our suits on and meet up in the kitchen. She grabs us a couple bottles of water on our way to the pool. After a few laps and splashing each other like children, we get out and lay on the side.

"Kristi, can I trust you with something? I have to get it off my chest, but I need you to promise me you won't over react. You can't do anything to jeopardize the safety of this person."

She looks at me with such sincerity "You can trust me with anything Jenna, and we can figure out together what is best."

I start slow and let her know without names what was going on in my first foster home. I tell her everything I saw personally and what was told to me by Bryan and Caden. She listens to every word, and processes it before speaking up.

"That is horrid, and I am so sorry you had to endure such things. If I were to tell Kathie, she would remove Caden immediately, but, like he told you there is no guarantee the next home will be better. Let me think on this for a bit, and I will let you know what I come up with. I promise I will not make a move without your approval." She says exactly what I wanted to hear.

"Thank you so much, Kristi. I can't tell you how much this means to me. My heart is so broken for this child. If you would have seen him when I left him you would understand. I tried so hard to give him so much happiness in such a short time. I was willing to live in that mess until I turned eighteen just so I could give him some sort of normal life."

I hug her and she tells me how beautiful my heart is, and that she will do what she can to help. "Oh, and one last thing, Caden has two younger sisters in other foster homes. Do you think we can find out where? I would really like to check on them to make sure they are okay."

She gives me a little wink. "I will do all I can, Jenna, but again, I can't promise anything."

I nod my head and smile. "I'll take that. It's better than nothing." We both head in to get showers so we can get dinner started.

After I finish my shower and give Angel a quick call. We talk for a few minutes but she is on her way to the movies with her new friends. I am happy she is having fun. It just makes me a little sad that she seems to have moved on without me. I can't expect her to put a hold on her life because of the nightmare I am going through. I am strong, and I will make it through this alone if I have to.

I go down stairs in search of Kristi, hoping I can help her with dinner. I find her in the kitchen chopping onions.

"Can I help with that? I really love cooking." She looks up at me and smiles.

"Sure you can. Would you mind chopping the bell peppers?" Yep, just like Mom.

"Oh, of course. That's easy." We work well together in the kitchen and have light conversation. We laughed and joked until John came in and Kristi's attention went to him and finding out how his day went. They both included me in their conversation, and we talked like a normal family. John excuses himself to get a quick shower so we can have dinner. Before he leaves he asks if he could to take us to a movie afterwards. That gets a full blown smile from me, and I clap my hands like a child. They both laugh at me, but I am too excited to care.

As soon as everyone is done with dinner, I hurry to get the kitchen cleaned so we can be on our way. I am craving some good hot, buttery popcorn and Red Hots. I know it sounds crazy, but, hey it's my craving. I run up to get my purse and make sure my hair is okay. I really need to get a haircut soon.

When I come downstairs, they are waiting by the door for me. John opens the door and waves us out. We pile into Kristi's new SUV John bought her for Valentine's Day. She told me he bought it just for her to be able to shop and not worry about how to get it all into the little trunk her Lexus had. I was surprised when Kristi told me this. My father would be just the opposite. He would buy Mom something with a smaller trunk, that way she wouldn't buy too much. I really think I am going to like John, too.

I have been here for over two weeks now, and I have no complaints. Kristi and John have been great, and I could not ask for better parenting. Kristi even let me take her car to Houston yesterday to meet Angel for dinner and bowling. Well, I didn't really bowl, but I watched her and Amy. Amy is her new friend from her job. She is really cool and seems friendly. They invited me to go water skiing with them today. Water skiing is my favorite thing to do and I would have loved to go, but I don't think it's a safe thing to do when you're pregnant. All in all, I had a great time with Angel. I really didn't realize how much I missed her until I had to leave, but I promise her I will come and see her every chance I get.

The trip home made me lonesome for Caden. I wish I knew if he was doing okay. I hope Bryan takes care of him like he did before. I will have to ask Kristi if she has figured anything out yet.

When I get home, Kristi is in the kitchen prepping for dinner. I'm in the middle of telling her how my day went, when John comes running into the house. "If y'all would like to see the birth of a new colt, hurry out to the barn. Butta is about to have her colt!"

I immediately answer yes, and Kristi dries her hands and follows us out. I hadn't noticed how big the ranch was until I went into the barn where they keep all the horses. We pass several horses before we make it to the mama horse they call, Butta. I peek in and see she is antsy about us being there, so I step back. Kristi and I watch from the door. John rubs her down to calm her. He talks to her like he would be talking to his wife. Butta seems to understand him, and before long she was pushing. John made his way to her backside as the two front legs start coming out. My stomach starts to growl, but I couldn't take my eyes off the miracle I was witnessing.

John watches as Butta starts pushing, and he grabs the colt's legs and begins to pull them. He continues to do this for about three minutes, when all of a sudden, Butta lays down in the hay. On the last push, the colt is out. Butta just lays there while John removes the water and sack from the colt's face. He rubs his gloved hands down the colt's nose to remove all the water. As John rubs its back, the colt turns its head to watch. I am amazed and can't believe I just watched a birth. John looks to Kristi and I and says, "It's a girl, who's gonna name her?"

Kristi looks at me with a big smile, "I have named the last thirty, honey, so this one is all yours."

I am in awe and spit out "Bella, can we name her Bella?"

John nods his head. "Bella it is. Happy Birthday L'il Bella." Oh my God, I just named a horse. I really named a horse Bella. I wonder if you can spoil a horse like you can a dog. I hope so because I plan on spoiling this one.

I wake up early the next morning, and hurry to get myself ready so I can go down and check in on Bella. When I get down to the kitchen, John is giving Kristi a kiss at the back door. "Oops. Excuse me! I am so sorry." They laugh at me. I wonder why they always laugh at me!

"No reason to be sorry, l'il lady. I can kiss my beautiful bride in front of God and anyone else. She's all mine."

My face must be as red as red could be. "Can I go out to see Bella now?" John waves me to follow him.

"Come on, I'll bring you in so Bella doesn't get defensive." I am hot on his heels.

"Okay, Jenna, when we go in, I need you to slowly go and pet Butta's neck. This will let her know you are no threat to her or Bella." When we go in, Butta eyes me so I go slow and rub her neck. She doesn't pull away, so I hope we are going to be friends. Bella rubs up on my leg and I put my hand on her head and give it a little scratch. She seems to like it.

John tells me. "It looks like they have accepted you, Jenna. I think it's safe to say you're welcome to come in at anytime to check in on them." One of the ranch hands come over. John introduces him to me and lets him know that I will be in to check on Butta and Bella. He asks that they keep an eye out for me. He nods and tells me if I need anything just come find him. I thank him and John as I walk back to the house.

"Well l'il lady, my work here on the ranch is done for today. I am going to catch a shower and head into the office. I can't wait until Bryson finishes up his degree so he can take over the family business. I sure am ready for retirement." He explains that his son has chosen to follow in his footsteps. Both Kristi and John talk so much about Bryson that I think I know him, and I haven't even met him.

After we have breakfast I am so uncomfortable. My clothes are getting way too tight. "Kristi do you know where I could find maternity clothes? All my clothes are extremely too tight."

"How would you like to take a trip to Houston? We could go to the mall and make a day of shopping. I don't have anything planned for today."

"Oh, Kristi! I would love that. Just let me grab my purse and we can go! Do you think we can stop by my house so I can get some money? It's not far from the mall, and it will only take a few minutes." She cocks her head to the side like she doesn't understand. "My Dad had money put up in the safe in case we needed anything, and didn't have the money in our accounts. All of Mom and Dad's accounts are frozen until I turn eighteen. I have been trying to be careful so I don't run my account too low."

"Jenna, honey, I have money and will buy the clothes you need. I get money each month to buy what you need or want. You save that money for later. With a new baby you will need it all."

Now it's my turn to look dumbfounded, "Oh, but that money should go for the food and electricity I use here, not my personal things. You have taken such good care of me. I can't ask you to pay for my clothes, too."

"Jenna, I am buying your clothes, and this is not up for debate. Now will you please get your purse and let's go do some shopping?"

We jump in the SUV and head out to Houston. She loves country music just like Mom and I did, so we sing and dance in our seats to our favorite songs. I swear my Mom has been placed in this woman's body. They are so much alike in certain things.

We have so much fun shopping. There was so much about maternity clothes I didn't know. She even talked me into a couple of breastfeeding bras. It has never crossed my mind to breast feed. Now I will have to google it and see if it's something I want to think about. Kristi said a breastfed baby is a healthy baby. God knows that's what I pray for everyday. I will speak to Dr. Lacy next week to see if she has some information I can read up on. Kristi even bought me shoes that will help with my back when I am farther along. I had no clue being pregnant was so complicated. I am so happy I have her, but I'm really missing Caden. Tonight after dinner I will ask her if she figured anything out. I want something done without having him moved to somewhere any worse than he is now.

Chapter 11

My phone rings and I run to the couch to see if I can find where I left it. "Hello? Hey, Mom sorry. I couldn't find my phone." She is excited and talking so fast I can't understand what she's saying. "Mom, please slow down and try that again." My Mom, all excited, is a trip.

"It's Butta, Bry. She..." Oh my God, not my horse! I will fucking freak out if something is wrong with my horse.

"What's wrong with Butta, Mom?" I can't believe...

"She had a colt, Bry. She's beautiful, and her name is Bella. Jenna named her Bella. Isn't that a beautiful name? You can change it if you want but, I think it fits her." My heart rate picks up and I laugh at how fast my mom is shooting off all this information without taking a breath.

"So, you're telling me Butta gave birth to a colt, and it's a girl? And you named it Jenna? Who is Bella?"

Mom laughs and laughs. "No, silly. Jenna is the foster child that is living with us, and she named Butta's colt, Bella." Wow I had that all crazy.

"How are they? I was hoping to be home before she delivered. I guess dad got the dates wrong. She was not supposed to be due for another week or so."

She explains it all to me and tells me she will send me pictures of them so I can see for myself that they are fine. She says Jenna watched the whole birth. Dad asked her to name it, and Jenna said she looked like a Bella. I like the name, but I don't know if I like a person I don't even know naming my horse. However, I don't say that to Mom. I can always change it if I want. Now I really can't wait to get home so I can make sure Butta is okay. This is her first colt. I guess this makes me a daddy. I laugh and think this is probably the closest thing I will get to fatherhood.

Ethan's detoxing was rough, but we all came out without a scratch. Ethan is doing well, and we have attended a few meetings together. He spoke out in the second meeting, and introduced himself as an addict. I was so proud of him, and just pray he keeps it up.

Once Ethan and I are done with our football shit, he, Ramie, and I will be Beaumont bound. Just a couple more days until I get to see my new baby, Bella. Maybe I will stay home more than three weeks. Some of my friends are planning a week trip to Galveston. I really want to go see if I can find a few hot ass women. I've had my fill of these childish college girls who think they are God's gift to men.

Ethan wants to take the bikes home with us, so later today we will get them loaded up on the trailer to haul them home. I will just ride to campus with him tomorrow. My mother has called everyday for the last week to keep me updated on Butta and Bella. Bella, I can't believe I have a horse named Bella. I guess it could have been worse like Skittles or Pancake. Then I would really have to hurt that little girl's feelings and change it.

I keep thinking of other names but, I know when I look in her eyes I will be able to tell what her name should be. That's how I named Butta. She reminded me of a butterfly when I was younger. Mom said I was trying to tell her a story about a butterfly and I was talking so fast. I started stuttering and said butta butta butta. So when I looked at her I wanted to call her Butta. My mom still makes fun of me for her name, but, hey, it was my horse to name.

Now that school is out and all football requirements are complete, I am more than ready to head home. I call Ethan and Ramie and ask if they are ready to hit the road. I have everything loaded except the ice chest with the food from the refrigerator. He said they're only three blocks away. I load the chest into the back of my truck, and lock up the house just as they pull up.

"Let's go, shit kicker!" I shake my head and stick Ethan the bird.

"Lead the way, shit stomper!"

Now, we're off, west bound.

What the hell are we stopping for now? Not even 10 miles out of Baton Rouge and Ethan's getting off the interstate. I follow him as he pulls into a Taco Bell. I should have known. Since his detox, the boy eats like a fucking horse. We park side by side, and I see Ramie jump out of the truck and run into the restaurant. "What the hell is wrong with her?"

He throws his hands in the air. "She has to pee again. I made her ass pee before we left the house. I told her she can't have anything to drink until we hit Lake Charles."

Why is she peeing so much? Now my mind is going ninety to nothing. I see her coming out so I ask her, "Hey, sweetheart, you want to ride with me and keep me company for a while?" She looks over to Ethan and he tells her its fine. She runs around the other side and hops in.

Once back on the interstate, I start a conversation about my mom having a new pregnant teen in her house to see if that gets her talking. I tell her what I know about her, which isn't much. Her reply was short and sweet. "To each his own!"

I ask her, "What is that supposed to mean."

"I don't plan on giving my milk for free. If they want milk, they need to buy the cow."

I laugh hysterically, I mean full on snorting. "What the fuck are you talking about girl? I didn't say shit about milk or cows." She looks at me like I just grew an extra head.

"If they want my pussy, they better marry me first. There is no way I am going to get pregnant for some fucking loser. Especially the one that is going to be dipping his dick into every girl he can. Then, when he can't, he will swing by my house for a quickie. No, not happening, not in this lifetime. My virginity will be given to the man that not only steals my heart he will have to treat me as his queen. He will have to be my forever. If he can't, then he can just keep stepping. I am not one of those girls that have to have a man to feel complete. I complete me for now, and my life is great."

Damn was I wrong on that assumption. Now I can breathe better. I was ready to get the name of the douche bag I was going to kill.

We make it to Lake Charles and pull over at restaurant called Steamboat Bill's. My parents have taken me here many times when we would visit my grandparents. The seafood here is off the chain. We wait to order before we head to a table. That's another thing about this place it's not all fancy. You can even seat yourself. We sip our drinks while we wait on our orders of boiled crawfish. Ramie ordered boiled shrimp because she says she can't eat anything that buries itself in the mud. I also put in an order to go. My mom loves their shrimp baked potatoes. This will be a nice surprise, and will keep her off my back. She is not happy that I stay away for so long. Hopefully, she will be too busy eating to fuss. Ha, there I go with my wishful thinking.

The three of us talk about our plans while we're home, and plan to get together for some fun. Ethan makes sure we will still attend meetings while at home. He wants to make sure he doesn't fall off the wagon. I understand where he's coming from. I was the same way for a few months. I assure him we will still attend meetings, and I am only a phone call away if he needs me. Ramie has decided to ride with Ethan so we don't have to stop for her to switch later. I give her a hug and kiss, and tell them to be careful and text me later. Here we go on our last stretch of Interstate before we are home.

Chapter 12

Jenna

After getting dressed to go help Kristi prepare for Bryson's homecoming. I come out of my room, and on the third step down. I look into the eyes of the most amazing, heart stopping, and breathtaking man I have ever seen. He's dressed in a black muscle shirt with the tightest pair of wrangler jeans, and a cowboy hat. His hair is coal black, and he must stand at least six two or six three. I stop dead in my tracks and stare at him. He says something, but I can't for the life of me make it out. "Excuse me?" I say in hopes he will repeat it.

"Nothing, darling, I was only thinking out loud." He says with a half cocked smile on his handsome face. My God who is this gorgeous man and where the hell he did come from?

Kristi comes out from behind him and waves me down. "Come down Jenna, I want you to meet my son, Bryson."

Oh. MY. GOD. I have to live under the same roof with this man for a few weeks? I don't think my hormones will be able to take it. I slowly come down each step, holding on to the rails to make sure I don't tumble down. When I reach the last step we are eye to eye, and he holds out his hand. I give him my hand, and he brings it to his lips and kisses it. It makes my knees so weak, I think I may pass out.

"Hello, little darling, it's nice to finally meet you." He has the most perfect Texas Cowboy accent I've ever heard. I take that last step down. My face is now at his chest. His chest is rock hard. His shirt looks like it is too small, and is stretched to the limit.

I finally get enough nerve to look up at him. Damn, he is looking down at me with that little tilt to his lips. At that very moment, my baby decides to do a flip in my stomach, and I grab it and let out a, "Oh, shit!"

He lets go of my hand, and Kristi shoots towards me. "Are you okay, Jenna? What's wrong?" I walk to the kitchen to find a seat to sit in before I fall. Lord help me with this one. Foster brother or not, this is one person that could take me places I couldn't even dream about.

"I'm fine. I think the baby just did one of those somersaults you told me they do."

Kristi looks scared, "Is this the first time you felt it move?"

"No, it's just the first time I felt it this hard."

Bryson takes a deep breath and ask, "Do you need some water or something, Jenna?"

"No, Bryson, but thank you. It just shocked me is all." John comes in about that time, looks at everyone around me and his eyes squint.

"Kristi is something wrong?" Kristi and Bryson turn to look at him and explain what happened. With relief in his eyes, he walks to Bryson, and they shake hands. Then give each other a tap on the back. "Glad to see you made it, son. I can't wait for you to meet Bella. She sure is a fine looking colt."

I see the big smile spread across his face and then he looks to me. "Yeah, I hear someone had the pleasure of watching my child being born and got to name her." He winked at me. Oh. My. God!

Now it's my turn to smile, "It was more than just pleasure. It was like a miracle watching her come out so alert. I was shocked when your dad asked me to name her. To me she just looked like a Bella. You can change the name if you don't like it. I would fully understand."

He laughs a little and says, "Let me get a look at her first, and then we will go from there." And I swear before God and all the saints, he winks at me again. I think I need to change my panties.

We go out to the barn so Bryson can meet Bella. He is so good with horses, and you can see the love he has for them. Kristi and John are happy he's home. You can see the love in their eyes when they look at him. I wonder how long he has left in college, and what his plans are when he's done. Maybe I can bring it up at dinner. That way it doesn't look like I am trying to get personal. I wish I would have listened to everything Kristi said about him since I arrived. I was not interested then, but now I want to know everything I can. I can't remember how old she said Bryson was. I would say at least twenty, and I'm pretty sure he has many women throwing themselves at him. There is no way he would have anything to do with me. Look at me I am underage, pregnant, and as big as a house.

Watching them together, I decide it's time to go back to my room so they can have time alone together as a family. As I open the gate to the back yard I hear footsteps running behind me. "Jenna, did I say something wrong? Where are you going?" I look over my shoulder and Bryson is standing with his hands on his hips.

"No, you didn't say anything wrong. I am just going to my room so y'all can have some family time alone."

He cocks his head to the side, "I don't believe that, Jenna. Something happened back there. I saw when your face changed, and I need to know why? Is it something we said or did that caused you to have a sad moment?"

What is he saying? How could he know? Did my face change that much? I try to play it off so he won't know I was thinking about him.

"I just felt you needed time with your horses and your family without me in the way, that's all."

"Well, if I am not mistaken you are now part of this family, now aren't you? You live here right? We share the same house and the same parents now, so I think that makes you family."

Damn he got me now, think Jenna. "I am only here for two months and they are only loaners until I turn eighteen, but they are *yours* and I am sure they want some time alone with you."

He presses his lips together and shakes his head. "I don't give a shit. Sorry for that. I don't care if you are here for only a week that means we have to share. Now, I want you to know you are not in anyone's way. You are welcome to be wherever we are." He tips his hat and goes back to the barn.

Oh, shit. Now he's pissed at me. All I wanted was for him to have time with his family. What is his problem? I will stay away because he is not going to make me feel like I did something wrong. I stomp up to my room and put my earphones in and lay across my bed. My belly is getting so big I can't see my toes over it. I am going to weigh a ton by the time this baby comes. I text Angel to see what's up with her and, as usual, she is out with Amy. This is going to be one long ass summer.

Kristi knocks softly on my door and asked if she could come in. "Jenna are you okay honey? Are you having more pains?" She is so sweet and always worried about me.

"I'm fine Kristi. I have no pains, just a lot of movement today." Which is true, this baby has gotten very active in the last hour or so.

"Can I feel it? If you don't mind me touching you, that is."

"Of course, come put your hand here." We sit there awhile and nothing, no movement what's so ever. "Bryson used to do the same thing when I wanted him to move for John." Kristi laughs at the memory. "We are going out to dinner tonight. We would really like it if you would join us."

I shrug my shoulders and put my head down.

"What's wrong Jenna? You know you can talk to me about anything honey." If anyone is going to understand me it's going to be Kristi.

"I just feel that with Bryson home, I need to step back. I should let you all have time together as family. You only get to see him a few weeks before he's gone again. I can fix myself something to eat here. You and John take him out, and enjoy your time together. I will be fine." I sure hope it doesn't hurt her feelings. I would never want to hurt her feelings.

"Jenna, honey, when I took you in it was to make you part of my family. When you turn eighteen and leave here, you will still be considered our family. We will always be here for you. You are not the first foster child in our home. Bryson is used to sharing us with them. We really would like for you to include yourself in the things we do. I won't force you to do anything you do not want to do, but please know we want you here. We want you to be a part of everything." The tears roll down my face. I forgot what it felt like to have a family. I hug her neck and thank her. I want to make sure she is not just being nice.

Bryson walks in when I am crying on Kristi's shoulder and immediately thinks the worst. "Mom, what did you do? What is wrong with her? I asked you to make sure she comes to dinner with us, not make her cry." He wanted me to go? What the hell. I told him earlier he needed time with his parents.

"Bryson, she didn't make me cry. Well, she did with the amazing way she has accepted me into this family. I just want you all to know, I am capable of staying alone. If you guys want family time alone I understand, really." He shakes his head at me again.

"Is this your room Jenna? Do you live here? Have you had dinner with them every night since you got here?" I nod to all his questions but he makes me look at him. "Answer me, Jenna."

"Yes, to all questions." Damn him.

"Then can you please put something nice on, and join us for dinner tonight? We are going to my favorite restaurant. I would appreciate it if you would accompany us." I am mesmerized by his eyes, I can't seem to look away, and neither does he. "Can you do that for me, please?" I nod my head again.

"Yes, I can, and thank you." He winks at me again and I melt. He walks out my door and Kristi speaks up. It seems I forgot she was there.

"Can you explain that to me, Jenna? Do you have a spell on my son?" We both laugh and she tells me she's going to get ready. We will be leaving in about an hour. I lock my door and hurry to the shower.

I'm all dressed and ready to go. I am so glad Kristi made me buy a few nice dresses. She said they were called, "just in case" dresses. Now I see where she got the name from. I spend a time long on my hair and makeup and, I keep going back to the mirror to make sure it's not too much. Why am I so nervous? I can do this. Please, Lord. Help me to do this without making everyone look bad. I grab my purse and open the door.

When I get to the stairs I see Bryson at the bottom step again. He's looking up at me with that smile. Damn, that smile can wet the panties of a nun. Get your shit together, Jenna. He's only being nice because you're his foster sister. When I reach the bottom, he asks if I am ready to go, and I nod my head. He puts his hand on my lower back and I swear the baby flips again. Why the hell does it keep doing that every time he touches me? I rub my belly in hopes that it will calm down.

He watches my hand and asks if everything is okay. I tell him yes, but the baby is very active today. "Can I feel it?"

I stutter but it finally comes out. "Ye, yess, sure." He puts his hand over mine. I move my hand and there it goes. Bam. Bam. Bam.

He smiles, "I think she likes me." She! Where the hell did that come from?

"She? We haven't found out the sex yet. I am hopeful that on my next visit it will open its legs so we can see." My last visit the baby refused to open so we could see. I think Kristi was more upset than I was. He just gives me another wink and leads us out to the car. What makes him think it's a girl? I really think it's a boy. We will see.

Meeting Bryson's friends Ramie and Ethan, was nice. They both seem to be good people. I think Ramie has an eye for Bryson, but I can't be sure. She seems to flirt a lot with him. The food was really good, all can see why it's his favorite place. They included me in everything, and I have to admit, I felt like part of the family. I was really afraid I would feel out of place and not have anything in common with them. They talked a lot about the fun they have at college. Angel and I had big plans to go away for college too. Well, now that I will have a baby going away is out of the question. I think a local college, or online college courses will be better with the baby. I just need to get through my senior year, and then I can think about what comes next.

Once we get home I go straight to my room. I am not sure why seeing Bryson hug Ramie and swinging her around made me so upset. I take a quick shower and lay in my bed. I need to contact Justin. I really need to tell him about the baby so I know what his intentions are. I don't need him, and I don't need his money. I would like to know if he plans on being part of the baby's life. I decide to call rather than send a text. A recording says it's no longer in service. I try again just to make sure. I get the same message. Oh, well, I guess that's my answer. I curl up and rub my belly telling my baby that we don't need a man in our lives, and we will be just fine.

I must have dozed off because I feel someone pull the blankets over me and rub my head. I just keep my eyes closed, but I hear him say, "Sleep little angel, I don't know what or who keeps making you sad, but I promise to protect you forever." What the hell does he think I need a bodyguard?. I wait until I hear the door close before I open my eyes. The baby is doing a dance in my stomach. Why does the baby get so active every time that man touches me? There is no way I will get back to sleep now. I grab the baby book Kristi insisted I needed to read. I open it and start reading, but my mind keeps wandering off to Justin. How on Earth am I going to find him?

I sneak in the driveway as quietly as I can. I told Mom it would be later today before I got in. I wanted to surprise her. Sneaking in the front door, I don't see anyone, so I figure they are upstairs. When I am about to take the first step, I look up and lose my breath. At the top of the stairs is the most beautiful little woman, with long flowing blonde hair and gorgeous blue eyes. She's wearing a white sundress with thin straps. Her cute little feet are bare. "My forever." When our eyes meet, she stops. I am so lost in her I hardly hear her say, "Excuse me?" Damn, I must have said that out loud. Think Bryson quick, "Nothing darling, I was only thinking out loud." No use in lying.

She smiles and I think I have just fallen in love. She looks like an angel up there sent here just for me. Who is she? Why is she coming from my room? Mom comes from behind me and introduces us. Oh. Hell. No. She can't be underage. She can't be my foster sister. Oh, fucking well. Foster sister or not, she will be mine. Three words strike my heart and I am shocked at even the thought of my heart waking up again. Love, Cherish, Protect. Play it cool, cowboy. She's only seventeen, and you will have to wait.

She walks slowly down the stairs, all in white. When she hits the last step, I put out my hand. I just have to touch her. I can't wait another minute. When her hand touches mine I feel the jolt throughout my entire body. I know I'm done, hook, line, and sinker. I kiss her hand because a handshake is not enough. She steps down, and her face is in my chest. She looks up at me and I smile. She grabs her stomach and says, "OH, shit", so I know she felt it too. Mom freaks out and comes to her side to make sure she's okay.

Why wouldn't Jenna be okay? What does mom think I did, bite her? "I'm fine. I think the baby just did one of the somersaults you told me they do." Oh shit the baby felt it too? Lord, if I ever needed your strength to be patient and wait, it would be right now. We go into the kitchen and she sits at the bar. Mom and I make sure she is okay and if she needs anything. Yes, she needs me but she doesn't know it yet.

Dad comes in the back door. He has a worried look on his face. Mom and I explain all is well and he relaxes. I give him a hug. Damn I missed the old man. He asked if I was ready to meet Bella. I am but I need to make sure Jenna is okay. I won't leave her now. I need to know she is alright.

"Jenna, what do you say we go out to the barn so I can meet Bella?" I want to see my new colt but I don't want to leave her side. All I can do is hope she accepts. She looks to Mom for approval and Mom nods. What the hell is that about? Does my mom have to approve her every move? I give her my hand to help her from the seat. We head out to the barn with Mom and Dad following.

When we reach Butta's stall, I start to talk to her. She looks around for me and starts shaking her head. "Hey, Butta girl. How's my girl? Where is the baby at? Show me girl." I open the door and the colt is immediately at my feet. I reach down and give her a good rub. I bend down and pull her face up so I can get a good look at her. "Yep, looks like a Bella to me, too. You did good Jenna." I see a smile creep up on her face and her little cheeks turn a pretty pink.

Oh, I plan on keeping them cheeks that color, or maybe get them to a bright red. Jenna comes in and rubs Butta and says a few words I can't make out. Once she is done, she sits beside Bella and tells her, "See I knew you were a Bella the moment I saw you. Now your daddy agrees too. So Bella it is girl. My Bella." I snicker at the mention of "her Bella". If she only knew how true that statement is. Jenna will soon be mine and so is Bella. How does that saying go, *"What's mine is hers and what's hers is mine!"*

I am watching Jenna with Bella, when this sad look comes over her face. I wonder what's wrong, but I don't ask. I am tending to Butta, but when I turn, Jenna is gone. Not sure what I did or said, I run after her. She says she is just giving us family time. Well, fuck family time. I want her with me. I let her go into the house, and I go back to the barn. It's time for Mom and I to have a talk. I ask, "Mom, what's the story on her? Why is she so sad at times?"

"Her parents were killed in a car accident. She has no other living relatives. She really has no one. She has mentioned a friend in Houston, her name is Angel. Other than that she's alone." That has to suck.

"What about the father of the child? Has he called or come by? Does he even care?"

"She hasn't said much on that situation, Bryson. I don't want to pry, but I'm sure she talk about it when she's ready."

Dad comes in and asks what I want to do for dinner. "I really would like to go out and eat at Red Lobster if you are all up for it? I can call Ethan and Ramie to see if they want to meet us there. I think Jenna and Ramie would get along well. I am sure she could use a friend." Mom agrees, so we make our way back to the house. "Mom will you go up and invite her, and make sure you don't take no for an answer?" Mom gives me the mean eyes. I know I will be answering questions later. I watch as Mom goes up to her room. I pace waiting for her to come out.

After about twenty minutes, I can't take it anymore, and I march my ass up to see what's taking so long. When I reach her door, I see Jenna holding on to my mom and crying. My heart rate picks up, and I think I am going to lose my shit. What the fuck has her crying? What did my mom do to her?

"Mom what did you do? What is wrong with her? I asked you to make sure she comes to dinner with us not make her cry." They both laugh at me and I don't know what the fuck they think is so funny about my girl crying. I don't see a damn thing funny. I make sure she knows we all want her to come. She is so headstrong. I like that about her. Mom and I leave her to get dressed.

I get a quick shower and I am dressed and ready to go, but I am the only one. I pace and pace, waiting for her to come down. After what seems like forever, her door opens. I stop pacing and look up. Damn, what a gorgeous, girl. Even her little baby bump. She is glowing like an angel you dream about at night. I smile and watch her come down. I can't wait to touch her. I put my hand on her lower back, and I'll be damned if I don't feel it again. I know she does too, because she grabs her stomach again. I was able to feel the baby kick. She kicked me three times. Jenna looks at me crazy because I said, "She" and says they don't know the sex of the baby yet. I do, and it's a girl. I give her a wink and watch her cheeks change colors as we head for the car.

I called ahead and made our reservations so we are seated when we come in. We have a table for six, and Jenna questions why. I let her know I have friends coming to meet us. Her face has that confused look again and I can't put my finger on the problem. Ramie and Ethan show up, and I wave them over. After I introduce them to Jenna, we they all take a seat. Dad orders a bottle of white wine to go with the seafood we are about to order, and Jenna orders an un-sweet tea with an extra lemon. Damn, why did Dad order wine when he knew she couldn't drink it? "I'll take the same please." If she can't drink, then I won't either.

The dinner conversation is mostly questions on how college is treating us. Jenna is listening, but you can tell she feels out of place. I don't want her to feel left out. "Jenna, are you planning to finish school?" She looks up with a smile and nods her head.

"I am. I will just have to hire a nanny to stay with the baby during the day. I also plan on going to college. My father had a very successful and productive company, which he sold six months ago. He invested over half and told my mother and I, we would have enough money that his grandchildren wouldn't have to work if they chose not to. I would really like to have a degree in case something was to ever go wrong."

Wow, I am blown away. I know I had no clue what I wanted for my future when I was seventeen. This girl has her shit together, and I can't help but tell her so. "Dang, girl. You got your stuff together. I am impressed." There goes the red I was looking for. But, as usual, Ramie hates when I make girls blush so she pipes in.

"Bry, stop making her blush you big bully." Jenna puts her head down and I catch her chin and get her eyes to mine.

"No ma'am, I will not let you hide that pretty face. I did not mean to embarrass you. I really am impressed, Jenna. I sure didn't know what I wanted out of life at seventeen."

She gives me that shy smile and I know we're back on track. The rest of the night goes well, and we are ready to go.

The waitress comes by and puts the check on the table, Dad and I both reach for it. Dad wins out only because I refuse to argue with him. Now, when Jenna pulls money from her purse to pay her portion, the gloves are off. I am ready to throw down. "Jenna if you don't put that money back in your purse, I am going to lose my shit right here." Her eyes go wide and she shakes her head.

"I have money to pay for my dinner. I don't expect you or your father to have to pay for me." I give her the look of a mad bad ass, but throw in a little half smile.

"You were invited, which means, we pay, and if you want to continue this argument, we can do it in the car." She puts her money away and thanks my dad then we walk out.

I saying goodbye to Ethan. Then give Ramie a big hug and swing her around. She giggles, but when I see Jenna's face go sad, I know she cares. I stop and put her down. I let them know I will be home for the weekend. I tell them I want to do some riding, and spend time with Bella. Ethan is not buying my shit, but he knows to keep his mouth shut until we are alone. Once inside the car, Dad starts talking about how things are going at Alexander and Associates. That keeps us going until we get home. Jenna is quiet and that make me nervous. I wonder if she was really jealous of Ramie?

Once we get home, Jenna goes straight to her room. I wait for her to come out, but she never returns. I ask Mom if that's a normal routine for her. Mom said she usually tells her when she is turning in for the night. I want to run up there but, I decide to let it go. She will come down when she's ready. I go out to check on Bella in hopes of getting Jenna off my mind. What is it about her that drives me crazy?

We have had at least thirty girls in this house before Jenna, and I never gave any of them a second look. I never wanted them around me like I want Jenna. Her smiles give me butterflies. Her sad faces make me want to kill someone. I need to talk to Mom. Fuck, what is wrong with me? Where is all this coming from?

I go back inside and have Mom go check to make sure she is okay. Mom comes down and says she is sound asleep. I tell her and Dad I am going to bed, and will see them in the morning. I pass her room to get to mine and can't help myself. I slowly open her door and there she is curled in a fetal position on her bed. Was she crying and fell asleep? What could have upset her? I guess I will have to wait until morning to find out. I pull the covers over her and rub my hand down her hair before I leave her.

Chapter 13

I have been here over a week now and have fallen into a routine of helping dad and tending the horses. I try to stay close to the house in case Jenna needs me. We talk every chance we get. I have to pull away at times so I don't give in to my cravings. Yeah, I said cravings. I crave her so much my body hurts. I love how she smells, and the way her hair flows in the wind. When Jenna smiles, the whole room lights up. Don't even get me started on that sexy ass voice of hers. Her lips, man I know want to know what they taste like. Damn, I know she's only seventeen, and I refuse to do anything with her until she is of age. Shit, I can't believe I two more long ass months before her birthday. I have taken many long cold ass showers, and have been able to talk myself down so far.

Ethan calls a lot and is always asking what is going on, but I am not sure what to tell him. How am I supposed to explain it to him? He and Ramie are planning to go back to Baton Rouge in four days. After talking to my dad I have made a decision to stay home. I haven't told them yet because I don't know how or what to tell them. All I know is that I am not leaving anytime soon.

It was a long night all I did was toss and turn. I walk into the kitchen and catch the tail end of a conversation between Jenna and Mom. Jenna needs to go somewhere, and mom can't take her. Jenna says she will just call her friend, Angel, to come get her. I am not comfortable with that, so I tell her I can take her. Jenna insists I will be bored waiting for her in a waiting room full of pregnant women. I make a joke on how I would definitely not be bored in a room full of women. All the blood drains from her face, and she races up to her room. I look to mom to see what I did.

"Bryson stop leading her on, you are very handsome and have a way with women. She is not seeing you as a brother, and I hope you know that." I don't see her as a sister either, but I can't tell her how I feel yet. For one I don't want to scare her off, and two she is underage.

"I was only joking mom, I don't mind taking her and I will wait for her to get done." Mom gives me that motherly look like I did something wrong.

"Then go up there and tell her so, and stop being a butt." I walk off shaking my head and go upstairs to talk to her. I knock on the door and ask, "Jenna? Can I come in?"

"Yes" she answers, so I open her door. I find her standing there brushing her long beautiful hair. I want to touch her. No. I have to touch her.

Holding out my hand, I ask, "Let me have the brush?" Jenna looks at me crazy but hands it over anyway. I brush her hair as I apologize for the joke down stairs.

"Jenna I was only joking. I will wait for you in the truck if that's what you want. I can come back with you so you can't lie when the doctor tells you we are having a girl." She turns her head so fast I think she may have whip lash.

"WE?!?"

I laugh and tell her, "Yes, we. Don't we have a bet on what it will be? And if I am not mistaken, we are your family. Now that means WE are having a baby, right?" Damn big slip up there. I have to be more careful.

She relaxes and says, "Okay. I am ready to go whenever you are.

Jenna and I head downstairs with smiles on our faces. I give Mom a kiss and we head out the door. I watch for a moment as Jenna tries really hard to climb all lady-like into my truck. It's not happening. I really need to put the steps on now that she will be riding with me. I lift her up gently placing her in the seat and belt her in. After I program the GPS we head for Houston. She laughs at my country music, so I turn it off. I figure this would be the best time for us to have a heart-to-heart talk. I start asking her questions, and she answers them. Some of her answers make me angry, but I really need to control my anger around her.

She tries to take the blame for that sorry son of bitch taking her virginity. I think I am going to lose my fucking mind. I will find this low life, and go with her to tell him about the baby. I will also tell him to stay the fuck away from both of them. She won't need him, because she will have me. Two more months, that's all I need to stake my claim on her and the baby. I just hope she agrees. Lord, please give me strength.

After answering all my questions, she now has free rein to ask me whatever she likes. I answer her honestly because I don't want any lies between us. It's over between me and Leah and has been for a year now. Telling her about Leah is not hard at all. Telling her I have been a man whore since the divorce is harder. The way I used women was so wrong. I am ashamed of myself now that I have to tell her that. Anyone before her was mainly just to get off .Once I have her, there will never be another woman for me. But I can't tell her that. I have to watch my words so I don't slip again.

"Are you hungry, Jenna?" I know she hasn't eaten since breakfast and I don't like her skipping meals.

"Not really, I'm too nervous to eat right now. Can I take a rain check, and we eat after my appointment?" I will take that, I have butterflies in my stomach, so I know she must be a mess.

"Sure thing little darling, and I will even let you chose the place since this is your hometown." The GPS says we have reached our destination. I park and tell her to wait for me to get her out of the truck. I jump out and run around to help her from the truck. Man, her body next to mine feels so right. I stare down in her blue eyes, and it takes everything I have not to kiss her. I grab her hand and we walk towards the building.

She signs in with the clerk, who is giving me, "fuck me eyes," and is told she can have a seat. We take a seat and I grab a magazine off the table next to us. I start flipping through, and I see a woman breastfeeding her baby. I hurry and flip pages and I hear Jenna snort. I look at her and she is trying so hard not to laugh.

"What's so funny?"

"You are." She must have seen me. Shit!

"Me? What did I do?"

She says in a low voice. "The look on your face when you saw that picture of the woman breastfeeding was priceless."

Damn, I was hoping she didn't see that. "Okay, so you caught me. Are you going to do that?" She shrugs her shoulders.

"I don't know yet. I talked to your mom about it and I am going to ask Dr. Lacy for some literature on it. Your mom says it's very healthy for the baby." I could handle her breastfeeding at home, but I just don't know if I want every man looking at my girl's tits. This is something we will definitely need to talk about.

The nurse calls her name and she squeezes my hand. "Do you want me to wait here or go back with you? It's your choice. I will be okay either way." She looks at me than the floor.

"I would like for you to come with me, but I don't want you to feel uncomfortable." Uncomfortable? Hell, I can't wait.

"I will be okay, and I would like to see her before everyone else does." That's really the truth. I can't wait to see this baby.

"Her? That's the third time you've said that, I am going to laugh when this baby has male parts." I laugh at that one.

"You keep dreaming my baby love, because this is my girl, I can feel it."

Jenna's eyes get wide but she doesn't say another word. They lead us to a room and take her weight and vitals. The nurse asks her if she has any questions. She shakes her head no and the nurse hands her a sheet. She also tells her to strip from the waist down, get on the table, and cover her lower half with the sheet. I ask her if she wants me to leave. She says I just need to turn around until she is done. I turn around but man, it's hard not to just sneak a peek.

Jenna lets me know when she's done, and I join her by the table to wait for the doctor. "Are you scared, Jenna?" She thinks a while.

"No, I'm not scared. I guess I'm just anxious to know what it is. I talk to it every night and I call it an "it", and I hate that. I am so ready to call it a he or she." I smile at her. She is so damn cute. The doctor walks in. Thank God it's a female. She asks how things have been going and she was glad to see Jenna had gained a few pounds.

"Are you ready to see what you're having, Jenna?" Jenna nods her head. The doctor squirts this blue shit on her stomach and moves this thing around her belly. Then, I hear it. My little girl's heartbeat is strong and steady. My eyes start to water. Dr. Lacy starts measuring different things and shows us the heart beating and then I see the head, arms, and legs. Oh, my God. It's our baby.

"What is it doc? I can't wait anymore." Jenna just looks at me and laughs.

"I think he is more excited than I am." The doctor points to something on the screen.

"Well, if you look right here I think it's safe to say this is a daddy's girl." I throw my hands in the air and pump them a few times.

"I knew it, I knew it." I look back and Jenna is crying, so I do the only thing that feels right, I kiss her. She puts her arms around my neck and cries.

"Thank you so much for being here with me, Bryson. It really means a lot to me."

Pulling back to look at her, I touch her face and say, "I would not have missed this for the world. Thank you for letting me be here, Jenna"

Dr. Lacy clears her throat, "I will print these up so you can have them. You can clean up and get dressed now, Jenna. I'll be back to answer any questions you may have."

Jenna's sweet little voice asks me. "Bryson, can you please tell me how you knew it was a girl?" I can't tell her, she will think I am crazy.

"I just had a feeling. You're so beautiful, it's only fair that you give birth to a baby girl that looks just like you." Damn there go the tears again. "Jen, please don't cry I can't take your tears anymore." I want to wipe away all her tears.

"But they are happy tears. I have been going through all this alone, except for when Caden was here with me."

Caden? Who the hell is that? She said the donor's name was Justin. "Who the hell is Caden?"

Jenna smiles. "Don't go getting all macho on me. Caden was the little boy in the last foster home I was in. He came with me on my last visit, and he held my hand. Caden is only twelve, but he tried his best to be the man I needed him to be. I will tell you all about him later." I am relieved, and a little jealous all in one, but I think I can live with it.

I give a smile, "Get that cute little ass dressed so I can get you fed."

"Fine, but you will need to turn around." Damn, I was hoping she would forget. I turn around and wait for her to finish getting dressed.

Dr. Lacy knocks, and comes in, handing me the printed pictures from the ultrasound. She talks with Jenna a bit about the vitamins, which are making her sick at times. Jenna also asks about breastfeeding. Then she breaks my heart.

"Bryson, would you mind stepping out a few minutes? There is something I need to talk to Dr. Lacy about in private." I don't understand what she has to talk about that I can't be here for. I let her hand go, and head for the door. The more I stand here in the hall, the more pissed I get, so I go out to sit in my truck. I turn on the radio, lay my head back, and try to process what I did to make her tell me to leave. Why would she want me out of the room?

Hearing a tap on my window several minutes later, I look down to see it's Jenna. I roll my window down and she asks if I could help her in. I get out and go around to open the door, and I put her inside. I hop back into the driver seat, and go to start the truck when she grabs my hand, "Bryson what's wrong?"

I turn and look into her watery eyes. "Nothing, Jenna."

She pleads with me to tell her, "Please, don't lie to me. I can see you're upset and I need to know why?" I need to tell her, but I don't want to sound like a dick.

"Why did you ask me to leave? What is so secretive that I had to leave? Is it because of him? Are you planning something behind my back? I have a million crazy things running in my head, and I can't seem to figure it out. Did I do something wrong?" Jenna's tears start to fall. Now I feel like shit. I start the truck, but turn to wipe the tears that are rolling down her chin.

"I had to ask her why my body wants you so bad, Bryson. I fight day and night with wanting you inside me. I know you're my foster brother, and I have tried to fight it, but I can't. My body needs a release. I had to ask her if that was normal or not. I'm sorry if I made you think you did something wrong."

Oh damn. Now I really feel like a dickweed. How do I respond to this? How do I tell her I have the same feelings? I pull her to me and hold her. "I'm so sorry, Jen. I didn't mean to make you cry. You have done really well hiding your feelings, so the thought never crossed my mind." Then she speaks the words I was not ready for.

"Bryson, you keep giving me mixed signals, and I don't know how to handle them. One minute you're acting like my big brother, the next minute you are flirting with me. Please, tell me what your intentions are, so I can deal with all these emotions I am having." Damn. I know I need to tell her. I just hope it doesn't scare her.

"Let's go eat and we can talk about it there, okay?" She nods her head. I make her buckle up. "Where we are going eat, beautiful?"

"I want a big fat, juicy steak. My favorite steak house is just up the road."

We pull up at Vic & Anthony's and she turns to me, "Just so you know Mr. Macho, I will be paying for lunch, since I lost the bet. If you have anything to say about that, say it now." I shake my head. I can't, or should I say, I won't argue with her.

I get out and come around to get her out of the truck. "I promise I will get the steps put on the truck this week so you can get in and out."

She smiles her sexy smile. That's fine, but a girl could really get used to a strong handsome man like you picking her up and helping her down." I hold her body up against mine, just so her feet can't touch the ground, so we are face to face.

"Well, in that case, I think the steps can wait a few more months." She throws her head back and laughs. I think I just heard my new most favorite sound in the world. I will do anything and everything I can to hear that sound as often as possible. I give her a quick kiss and set her down on her feet. After locking the truck, I take her hand and we walk to the door. Why does this just feel so right, when I know the rest of the world thinks it's wrong because she's not eighteen?

We have a long talk while eating, and Jenna tells me all about Caden and the family she was with. How can I hate people I have never met? Hate comes easy because these people hurt my girl. She misses Caden, and I try to figure out how I can get her to see him without anyone getting in trouble. She mentioned Bryan works at the local grocery store. Maybe I can reach him there. I know I will figure out something. She also wants to find this fucking dick that got her pregnant. She wants to put that behind her too.

When I try to pay the ticket, she insists she pay it. I agree, but I let her know I am paying tonight. I am taking her to dinner and a movie. She needs to get out more, and I plan to help her with that.

Once we get home we find Mom and Dad. "Well, Mom it looks like we won. It's a girl!" Mom and I won the $100.00 bet so we are planning to buy something for the baby with the money. I tell Dad about Vic & Anthony's and how he would love their steaks. He tells Mom he would like to try it one day soon. Jenna says she is going up to lay down a while, and send a text to Angel to let her know all about the baby.

I ask Dad if I can use his office because I have a few things I need to take care of. Dad tells me that office is just as much mine as it is his. I love my dad and he has so much confidence in me. He is so ready for me to take over the company, so he and Mom can enjoy his early retirement. I snatch a bottle of water out of the fridge, and make my way to the office. It's time to get things done and behind Jenna so she is not so stressed.

Finding the number for the store where Bryan is employed was easy. I make the call and am happy that he was the one that answers the phone. I explain who I am, and why I'm calling. He immediately asks how Jenna is doing, and if he can speak to her. I let him know she is fine, and I want to surprise her with a visit from Caden. He agrees, and thinks it will be a great surprise. Bryan says that Caden is having a hard time being away from Jenna as well. We plan it for Friday, since he is off. They will meet us at a park not far from the ranch. I hang up and feel good about what we have planned. I know Jenna will be so happy to see Caden.

Jenna

Morning comes quick since I hardly slept. I hear movement in the kitchen, and I jump out of bed and get dressed. I want to see Butta and Bella. I didn't do my nightly visit before bed last night, and I am really missing them. John and Kristi are having their coffee when I come down. Kristi offers to make my coffee milk. I let her know I am going to check on the girls first. I head out to the barn and start calling Bella's name as I enter. This gets her excited and waiting for me when I get to their stall. I can hear her little hoofs against the door. I open it up, and she rubs her nose on my legs.

"Spoiling her much?" I grab my heart, and spin around to find Bryson standing there with his arms crossed.

"My God, Bryson. You scared the shit out of me! Yes, I do spoil her. I watched her come into this world, and I have been there every day since." Chuckling, h,e pushes himself off the post and comes towards me.

"I was only joking Jenna. You can spoil her all you want to. I will break her when the time comes." What does he mean break her? He is not going to do any such thing. I will go to John if he tries to hurt her.

"What do you mean?"

He laughs, "Your face looks like I just told you I was going to kill her. I only said break her. That means when it's time to train her I will get her out of the spoiled stage. I would never hurt her or any horse. Please get that look off your face, Jenna." Thank God. I stick my tongue out at him and get the brush so I can brush Butta down. He grabs my sides and starts to tickle me. I beg him to stop and he wants me to say uncle. I finally give in and say it.

"Come on girly, let's get you and that baby some breakfast before Mom comes looking for us." We lock up and go in the house for breakfast.

John gives me a smile and asks, "Jenna, do you know how to ride horses?"

"I rode horses with my grandfather when I was younger. My grandfather had a couple of horses he used when he had things to do on the farm."

"Would you like to go for a ride today? Bryson and I could saddle up four of the horses and we could make a day of it."

Kristi chimes in and says, "John, she's pregnant! Are you crazy? Would you have let me get on a horse while I was pregnant?" John shakes his head and apologizes to me for forgetting, but says I am welcome to come back after the baby is born. I let him know it's okay, and if not for Kristi saying it was not a good idea, I would not have realized the danger.

Things go well for the next week or so. Bryson doesn't leave much and if he does, he always offers to take me with him. Sometimes I go, other times I stay home with Kristi. Today I have a doctor's appointment and will hopefully find out what I am having. We are all betting on what it is. Kristi and Bryson say it's a girl, while John and I say it's a boy. We all put up $25.00, so the pot is just waiting for the answer. I come out of my room and ask Kristi if she is able to take me to Houston for my appointment.

She grabs her head and says, "Oh my God, Jenna, I forgot today was your appointment. I promised I would take my father to see his sister in the hospital in Louisiana. I am so sorry." What am I going to do now?

"It's okay Kristi. Maybe I can call Angel. I am sure she wouldn't mind coming to get me." Bryson walks around the corner.

"Get you for what?"

"I have a doctor's appointment today in Houston, but your mom has other plans and can't take me."

He smiles and winks at me, damn him. "I can bring you. I have no plans for today." Great this is all I needed, to go into the doctor's office with wet panties.

"Thanks, but are you sure? You can just drop me off and I can text you when I'm done. I would hate for you to be bored in the waiting room with a bunch of pregnant women." He laughs and comes back with what he thinks is funny.

"A room full of women don't sound boring to me, little darling."

I feel my face change colors and head to my bedroom. Why do I let him do that to me? He can have who he wants, but he doesn't have to talk about it in front of me. My hormones are crazy, and the more I am around him the more I want him. I know this is crazy, and sex was never a problem before for me, but this past week and a half, I think I am going to lose my mind if I don't find a release. I plan on talking to Dr. Lacy today to see if this is normal.

Kristi hugs me and wishes me luck as we walk to the truck. Bryson's truck is so high he has to help me in, which means he has to touch me. Once inside he pulls my seatbelt across me and makes sure it's secured. I wave to Kristi as we drive off. The music is playing and I can't believe he likes country music. I smile and wonder what other things he likes. "You want to let me in on what has you smiling like the cat that ate the canary?" Does this man miss anything?

"Just didn't have you pegged for country music, that's all."

He smiles, "I like all music, but country music is relaxing. After a divorce you tend to find a lot of the songs seem to touch home. We can change it if you want, or we can turn it off and talk?" Talk? What does he want to talk about?

"Talk about what?" He laughs again and I wonder why everyone is always laughing at me.

"Well for one, I would like to know about your boyfriend?"

Whoa, who said I had a boyfriend? And why would he want to know about him?

"I don't have one." He looks at me from the corner of his eye and then looks to my belly. "Oh, you mean the baby's father? Well, there is not much to tell. We were together one time and I got pregnant, end of story." Now let that sink in for a while.

"Do you love him? Is he going to be a part of the baby's life? Is he going to marry you?" I look down at my hands in my lap, not sure of what to say or how to explain it to him.

"No, I don't know, and no." I really don't.

"Can you elaborate a little?" What does he want me to tell him? Justin won't answer me.

"No, I don't love him. He took my virginity at a weak moment, and I got pregnant. We never discussed love. I don't know if he plans to have a part in the baby's life. He has never answered my texts or calls since that night. Now, his number has been disconnected. And, as far as marriage goes, I would never marry him just because of the baby. When and if, I marry, it will be because I have found the perfect man who will love me for me. That person would also have to love my baby just as much. I may never find that person, and may be single for the rest of my life." I wait for what comes next. He can have all the questions he wants, but he will be returning the favor. There are many things I want to know about him, too.

"What is his name, and how old is he?" Why does he want to know this?

"Justin Hamilton, and he is twenty-one." He looks at me like I just grew a new head.

"Twenty-one? Did he know you were underage?"

"I don't know if we ever discussed my age. We talked about his family and his job, you know, things like that. I don't want you to think the worst of me. Like I told you, I was a virgin. My car wouldn't start one day when I was at the mall. He came by and asked if I needed help. He got my car started, and asked if we could have dinner. I figured I owed him that much. After dinner, we exchanged numbers. I hadn't heard from him in like two weeks when I got a text."

He said he really needed someone to talk to. I lied to my parents, and told them I was going to dinner with Angel. I met him in a parking lot not far from my house. I got in the car with him, and we were supposed to just go for a ride and talk. He started telling me that he and his sister had gotten into a big argument, and he told her some really hurtful things. She took off in her car and got into a really bad accident and was killed. Now, he was blaming himself. I tried to comfort him and tell him it wasn't his fault. That's where he took advantage of my sympathy, and I let him. Now ,here I am with his baby."

167

I can't see Bryson's eyes, but his lips are pressed together so hard they are turning colors. I just sit and wait for his reaction. I have a feeling this is not going to end well.

"So he never asked your age, nor did he ask permission to take you to bed?" I shake my head no. He hits the steering wheel, and I jump. "Where does he live Jenna?" Hell, no. This is not happening.

"I don't know Bryson. If I did, I would have gone there to tell him about the baby. But I don't know." Now he is the one shaking his head.

"I will find him, and when I do I will teach him a few things about how to treat a lady."

"You can't do that. I am just as much to blame as he is. I let it happen. I was the stupid one that didn't stop him. All I wanted was to take away his pain, so I let him. Please, promise me you won't get yourself in trouble because of me? I would never be able to forgive myself, Bryson. Please, promise me now." My tears begin to flow, and I dig in my purse for Kleenex. He hands me a napkin from the glove compartment.

"Please don't cry Jenna, I promise I won't provoke a fight. I will find him for you, on one condition. I go with you to tell him." I agree because it's not something I want to do alone. I just want to tell him, so I can move on and start a life for me and my baby. I thank him for caring about me enough to take up for me.

He smiles and says, "So I see you're into older men!" I flip my head towards him and he gives me that wink. Bam, panties wet again. Lord, please let me get to Houston before I climb on his lap. Damn these hormones!

At the doctor's office, we find out what the baby is. I ask Dr. Lacy a few questions, and then I ask Bryson to leave the room. There is no way in hell I am going to ask her about my horny ass in front of him. He looks mad, but I am not sure at what. After I am done with Dr. Lacy, I walk back into the hallway and Bryson is not there. I assume he has gone to the waiting room, but he's not there either. I head to the truck, and I can hear his music from the front door. I go to the truck to get in, but my side is locked so I have to go to his side to get his attention. He rolls down his window and sees it me. He puts me in the truck, without even belting me in and shuts the door. Damn he is mad.

I ask what's wrong but he only says nothing. I feel bad that I have put him in this mood, so of course my hormones kick in and I start to cry. Finally, he tells me he's upset because he doesn't understand why I asked him to leave the room. He thinks it has something to do with Justin. Not wanting to tell him I am a horny toad, I try to find the right words.

"I had to ask her why my body wants you so bad. I fight day and night wanting you inside me. I know you're my foster brother and I have tried to fight it, but I can't. My body needs a release. I had to ask her if that was normal or not. I'm sorry if I made you think you did something wrong."

I see the hurt in his eyes, and he drags my body to his side of the truck and holds me. Didn't I just tell him I wanted him? Didn't I just tell him I am fighting not to jump his damn body? I tell him what I want to eat and that I am paying, so we head to Vic & Anthony's for a fat juicy steak. He takes my hand as we walk to the door. Can anyone tell me why this feels so right?

Chapter 14

I need to find Justin Hamilton. I google him and find out very little. I decide to see if I can find him on Facebook. I do a search, and more than one comes up. Next, I go by Houston as the hometown, then by age. Bingo, I find him and start reading things he has posted. My blood starts to boil. One post reads, *"I am so excited I am going to be a daddy. The love of my life has said yes to my proposal, I couldn't be happier at this minute."* I am so mad! How could she have fucking lied to me to my face.

I storm out of the office, and up the stairs to her bedroom. I don't even knock, I just walk in. She raises her head and looks at me. "Why the hell did you lie to me, Jenna?" Her mouth falls open and she is lost.

"What do you mean lie to you? I have never lied to you about anything." That just pisses me off more.

"Really? You told me Justin doesn't know about the baby, and that you were never in love with him. Yet, I find the son of a bitch on Facebook and his post says he's marrying the love of his life because he is going to be a father. Care to explain that, Jenna?"

Tears well up, and I am too mad to care. "I told you I have never gotten to tell him anything about the baby. As far as marriage and love, that is completely out of the question. Can I please see the Facebook?" I grab her hand, and I take her back to the office.

"Here, it's all there." Jenna reads it, then scrolls down his page, and pictures pop up of him and another pregnant girl. She keeps going, and an ultrasound picture pops up that says, *it's a boy.*

She turns to me and says, "There are your answers, Bryson. Thanks for not believing me."

She tries to go around me, but I catch her and sit her on Dad's desk. "I'm sorry, Jenna. I just saw that post, and I lost it. I thought you were playing me. Ever since my ex did what she did to me, I have trust issues. I'm really sorry. Please forgive me?" She puts her head down and starts to speak to me.

"Bryson, I have no reason to lie. I have no one in this world except my baby. You and your parents are the closest thing to family I have, besides Angel. Why would I lie and jeopardize that?"

I wrap my arms around her and whisper in her ear. "I'm so sorry, baby. Please forgive me. I promise, I will never jump to conclusions like that again. I am just so damn jealous. I can't wait to get Justin out of our lives." She in turn whispers back in my ear.

"You're forgiven this time, but please, don't call me a liar again. As far as Justin is concerned, he is out of our lives already. I just need to get him to agree to give up his parental rights to the baby." I squeeze her a little tighter and then let her go.

"I have his address. Are you ready to see him?"

"Can I have a few minutes to get ready?"

"Sure, you can. How would you like to go out to dinner and a movie once we get this mess out of the way?"

"That sounds awesome, Bryson. I will hurry, I promise." She heads up to her room while I go to tell Mom we won't be here for dinner. I also let my mother in on my plans with Bryan. She gets excited and says she can add to that surprise. She says we will talk later and tells me to be careful on the road.

Justin lives in Baytown. I put the address in the GPS and we set out. I start some small talk to break the silence. "So, do you have any names picked out?" She shakes her head and tells me she thought it was going to be a boy, so she hadn't really thought about girl names. I smile, and I finally decide to ask the question that has been weighing heavily on my mind.

"What are your plans after your birthday?" She starts picking at her fingers, and that makes me nervous. I grab her hand and hold it in hopes that it will help her feel more comfortable.

"I guess I will go home and get everything ready for when the baby comes. I have lots of shopping to do, and a lot of things to learn before she makes her grand entrance. Angel and her mother are only a few houses down. I am hoping they will be able to help me, too."

This is not the answer I wanted to hear. I wanted her to tell me she is staying with my parents until after the baby is born. I need to talk to my mom. We can't let her go home alone. She needs us to help her take care of a new baby. Who the hell will take care of her?

"Have you even given any thought on staying at the ranch, so we can help you? I mean, this is your first baby, and you don't even know what all comes with being a mom. Who will take care of you? You will need help with cooking, cleaning, and getting out of bed at night. Who will help you bathe, and take care of all the things that will need to be done for the baby?"

She tries to pull her hand from mine. "No, Jenna. Don't pull away, I am only asking. I know my mom would love to have you stay until you are back on your feet, and know what to do. Please, just think about it, okay?"

"Okay, I will think about it, but Bryson, I heard you on the phone with Ethan yesterday. I know you are pushing your friends away to help me. That makes me feel bad. I am not your problem. I refuse to let you sit here in case I need something. You really need to go on with the plans you guys made for the summer." I rub the stubble on my face and make sure the words come out right when I tell her what I have to say.

"Jenna, first of all, you are not a problem and I never want to hear that come out of your mouth again. Second, I spend most of my time with Ethan and the gang back at college. Third, I want to spend time with you. I want to be around you. I want to help you resolve things. I can't explain it all right now, but I will soon. The only thing I can tell you is, we both have the same feelings. I fight day and night, just like you, to keep my hands off you. I know you said I send you mixed signals, and I don't mean to, but I can't help it. I am trying to do the right thing here, and wait the few weeks we have left until you are eighteen. Please, don't push me out now. We can call it whatever you want. I can say it's the big brother protector in me that wants to save you from any harm. In the end, my heart knows better, and so do you."

Jenna, takes off her seat belt, picks up the armrest, and slides next to me. She finds the new seat belt and puts it on. I put my arm around her, as she rests her head on my arm and chest. Oh, my God, this feels so right. I kiss the top of her head, and drive the rest of the way with a full heart and smile.

When we pull up to Justin's house and Jenna immediately recognizes his car. I'm glad to know we are in the right place. "Do you want me to go with you, or would you prefer to do this alone?"

"I would like for you to be there if you think you can hold in your anger. I just want to tell him, and be out of here as soon as possible."

I promise her I will keep my cool as long as he respects her. I silently thank God, because I would go crazy sitting in this truck not knowing what's happening out there. She rings the doorbell, and we wait. Soon, a tiny woman with a very large pregnant stomach, which if I had to guess I would think she is due any day now, opens the door.

Jenna introduces us both and asks if Justin is in. She invites us in and calls out to Justin. When he comes around the corner, he stops in his tracks with a shocked look on his face. I decide to step up and save his ass. "Hey Justin, I am Bryson Alexander, and this is my girl, Jenna. I was wondering if we could have a word with you outside." Now, hopefully he doesn't do anything stupid to mess it up. I am only doing this to protect the two pregnant women who don't need any added stress.

Nodding, Justin leads the way out. The three of us walk towards my truck. When we are out of earshot of his girl, he turns and asks, "What are you doing here, Jenna? What is this all about?"

Jenna speaks up and takes over the conversation. "Justin I have been trying to get a hold of you for a couple of months now."

His smart ass remark was enough for me to want to punch his lights out. "I know, that's why I changed my phone number. I don't want to have anything to do with you, or that child. How can you even say it's mine anyway?"

I stand a little straighter, and move a little closer with both fists ready to fuck up his face. Jenna takes her finger and pushes it in his chest.

"Because YOU are the only person I have ever been with. You took my virginity that night, and I have not been with anyone else since. You knew this because there was blood all over your seat that night. Don't play stupid with me, Justin! I am here to ask you to sign over all your rights to her. I also want to ask that you never try to contact her or me in the future. If you agree, we will walk out, and you never have to see us again." Damn, I am so proud of Jenna, I swear she is such a strong person to have dealt with all the shit she has in the past few months.

Instantly he says, "Where do I sign?" I breathe deeply, and relax just a little. Now, it's my turn to step up with all the legal information he will need.

"I will have my lawyer draw up the papers, and someone will be contact you to have you sign them. If you want, I can call you with a day to come into his office to sign. I will need your number to contact you. I will delete it whenever all the paperwork is done, and you will never hear from either of us again." He says he will come into the office because he doesn't want his fiancé to find out. Before we leave, Jenna has one more question.

"Justin, did your sister really die in a car accident?"

He looks her dead in her eyes and says, "No, but my plan sure worked, huh?"

I lunge at him and Jenna begs me to let him go because he is not worth it. I shove him and let him know he is a sick individual, and he will answer for this one day. I put my arm around my girl and lead her to the truck. I put her in on my side because I need her next to me. I need to know she is okay.

Jenna puts her seatbelt on and turns to me, "Thank you for being here with me. I don't think I could have done that without you." I bring her head close to me and kiss her hair. There are no sign of tears, but I know that had to hurt her.

"I am glad I was here for you. I am so happy that it is all over now. If you need to cry, I understand. I want to be here for you.

She looks up at me and says, "I have no reason to cry. I didn't love him. I just wanted to be able to tell my child that her father knew about her. She will know it was his decision to give away all rights to her." I turn my body so we are facing each other.

"Jenna, I am going to ask you something, and I know you are not expecting this. It may shock you, but please know, I am serious, and I have never been more serious about something like I am now."

Jenna nods and waits, and I take her face in my hands, "That low life piece of trash just gave you all of his rights as father to your daughter, and they are now yours. What I want to know right now is if I can please have those rights? Can I be her father? I promise, I will never let her or you down. I will be the best damn father in the world to her."

She is shocked and the tears are rolling down like rain. "Bryson, I can't ask you to do that. You have your life to live. I can't let you throw that away and marry me. Being a father to a child that is not yours is not fair to you. Bryson, I want to marry a man who will be so madly in love with me he will see no other woman besides me." My throat feels like a desert it's so dry. I need her to know I have thought about it all.

"Jenna, baby, do you not see how much you mean to me? Do you remember the first time I laid eyes on you, I said something and you said excuse me?"

She nods her head. "Yes, and you told me you were just thinking out loud."

"Yes, but what I said was, 'MY FOREVER'. You are my forever, Jenna. I knew it the minute our eyes met. I never wanted to love again. I never wanted to let anyone back into my heart, until I laid eyes on you. I just have to wait until August to let the world know that I love you. I want you and this baby, our baby, in my life forever. I don't want people to look down on us because you were underage. I want everything to be right, so no one can ever take you away from me." She unbuckles her seatbelt and straddles my lap. She holds my neck so tight it's hard to breathe. I hold her as tight as I can without hurting her or the baby.

We stay like this for as long as I can take it. "Jenna, baby, if you stay like this any longer my zipper is going to burst. I am really close to taking you in my truck. Believe me I would much rather have you in a bed for our first time than here in my truck." She giggles and slowly gets off my lap. I try to fix my dick so I am not so uncomfortable, but I can't seem to make that happen. Even thinking of fat women in string bikinis is not helping. I start the truck and ask her where to go next. She lets me know she is done, and the rest of night is mine. I want to get her back to Beaumont, and as far away from this place as I can.

Jenna

Once Bryson and I return home from seeing Dr. Lacy. I go upstairs to lie down, and call Angel to give her the news. I am dozing off when my room door swings open and in comes a mad Bryson. He accuses me of lying to him about Justin. I am not sure I understand where he gets off calling me a liar. He takes my hand and leads me to his dad's office and shows me the computer. I see its Facebook and the picture is of Justin. He points to the post he is speaking about. I read it, and yes, it says he is marrying the love of his life and she is pregnant. But, I am not that girl, and I need to give him proof.

I scroll down and low and behold, there it is, a picture of the two of them together. I see Bryson's face change, but I don't say a word, I scroll down more and come up on an ultrasound picture and it says *"it's a boy."* Now, I turn to him and all he can say is "sorry". I really don't want to hear it right now. He didn't have enough faith in me to believe me when I told him the first time. Why should I give him this?

I go to leave and he picks me up and puts me on the desk. My poor body is on high alert as it is. Now, with him putting me here like this it sends it into extra high alert. Like that's not enough, he begins whispering in my ear. I swear I just came in my pants. I decide an eye for an eye. I whisper back to him. We make up and he says he has the address for Justin, and that we can go now. I run up and get ready. I am so ready to get this over with.

Seeing Justin did nothing for me. I just wanted to tell him what I had to say in hopes he will give up his rights. Bryson was awesome, and handled it like a pro. I would have just told him in front of his woman. Bryson was more adult about it, and had him come outside. He agreed to sign his rights over. The only thing that made me angry was when I asked him if he had lied about his sister being dead, and he admitted it.

He told me it was his plan to get into my pants and it worked. I had to beg Bryson to let him go because I don't want him to go to jail because of me. Bryson also finally came clean with me about his feelings towards me. It was a shock, but also a relief. I thought I was the only one with the crazy feelings. He also asked me if he can have Justin's rights as the father of my baby. I didn't give him an answer, yet, but I did give him a hug. Bryson says this is what he really wants. I want it too, but I am afraid he is not ready for a baby. Not to mention a baby that's not even his own. I will give him more time to think it over. I will not hold him to anything. This is my baby, and I will do what's best for her.

Chapter 15

"Are you still up for dinner and the movies, Jenna?" She says she's not that hungry, and would rather eat some popcorn and Red Hots at the theatre. That really sounds gross, but if that's what she wants, I am all for it. I even let her chose the movie. Of course she chooses a chick flick but that's just fine with me. I will watch Cindafuckingrella if it makes her happy.

After getting everything we need at the concessions counter, we make our way into the theater to find our seats. The movie is not as bad as I thought it would be. About half way through it Jenna, says she needs to use the ladies room. I hold her popcorn and water as she hurries off. After about fifteen minutes, I am getting really nervous because she is not back yet. I put everything on the floor, and go in search of her. We meet up just inside the theatre door and I ask if she is alright.

"I am not feeling well. Can we please just go home?" Should I take her to the hospital or call Mom?

"Sure, let's go. Do you need to see the doctor?" She won't look at me.

"No, I just need to get into bed, and I will be good." I go to take her hand so we can go, but she pulls her hand away and puts it on her stomach. I wonder what is wrong, but figure maybe the damn Red Hots and popcorn has upset her stomach. When we make it to the truck, she goes to her side, not mine. I help her in and she belts herself in. At this point, I do not like this situation at all. Something is wrong and she's not telling me. On the way home, I am extremely worried about her, but she keeps saying she will be fine. She won't even look at me. Something is wrong, and I plan on finding out what it is.

Once we are home, Mom asks why we are home so early. I let her know Jenna is not feeling well and wants to go to bed. Mom just smiles and explains that this is normal for a pregnant woman. I relax a little and tell Mom I am going to catch a shower and relax in my room. It's only a little after seven and I am not tired, but I am really worried about Jenna. I knock on her door before I walk in, and she is curled up in her bed. I make my way to her and kiss her head. "Sleep well, baby, and I am right next door if you need anything, okay?" She says okay, and I leave her room.

After taking a quick shower, I lay in my bed and shoot a text to Ethan. He answers right away, and says he is bored, too, but no one wants to go do anything. He starts asking questions about Jenna, and I know he sees through me. I won't try to deny it. I ask him if he wants to meet me in the barn. He replies, "Hell, Yeah!" and I slip my jeans and boots back on, grab my hat and undershirt then head down stairs. I grab a Coke from the fridge before heading out to the barn.

I stop short when I hear a soft voice talking. I creep up to Butta's stall. I can hear her telling the horses she has to get out of here. What the fuck does she mean she has to get out? Where will she go? I'll be damned if she is leaving here. I listen to see what else she says.

"The woman says she loves him, and he loves her, so I had better stay away from him or something bad is going to happen to me and my bastard child. I'm so scared Butta, I don't know what to do. I can't take the chance of telling Bryson. What if she tries to kill me and my baby? I think I just need to call Kathie to get me out of here."

Who the hell wants to kill her? I don't know the answers, but I am about to get them. I clear my throat and walk into the stall. "Hello, Jenna. I think you have some explaining to do." She shakes her head and swears she can't and won't. I move in and reach for her hand.

I tell her, "You can, and you will. If you're in danger, I need to know. Who is she, and where did you talk to her?"

Her body is trembling. I pull her into my chest to soothe her.

186

"Jenna baby look at me. You need to tell me who told you this. I swear to you, I will not allow anyone to hurt you. Just tell me who and where, please?" Her lip begins to tremble and I want to so bad to pull her to me but I don't. She needs to tell me so I can stop this now.

"Tonight, at the movies I went to the restroom. When I came out of the stall she was at the mirror and she told me you belong to her. She said you love her, and that I could never have you. She said if I didn't leave you alone she would kill me and my bastard child."

I pull her to my chest once again, "Fucking Leah." I will kill that bitch if I see her anywhere near Jenna. I didn't see her at the theater, how did I miss her? Is she stalking me again? I pull out my phone about the same time Ethan arrives at the barn. God knows what he's thinking now. "Don't jump to conclusions. This is not what you think." He holds his hands up and shakes his head.

"Hey, Bro. You know I don't get in your business. I am just here because I needed someone to talk to." Jenna tries to pull out of my embrace but I hold her tighter.

"Bryson, just let me go, I can't stay here. I won't put my baby in danger. I will just call Kathie to have me placed elsewhere. I don't want to cause problems for you and your girlfriend." What the hell is she talking about? I don't have a girlfriend. Jenna is not going anywhere without me. I look to Ethan for help, and he is laughing.

"What the hell is so funny, dude?" I want to throat punch him right now.

"You having a girlfriend is what's so funny. Didn't anyone tell her you don't do relationships?" Now I want to bash his face in. This is not what she needs to hear right now. I glare at him and he knows.

This time Jenna squirms out of my hold and runs out of the barn. I start out after her when Ethan grabs my arm. "Let her go, bro. You hurt her enough. Think about her mental state, and give her a break. She needs stability, and you are not the person she needs."

I glare at him, "Get your fucking hands off me. You have no idea how I feel and what I am capable of being." I jerk my arm from him and go in search of Jenna.

I find her sitting by the pool in the dark. "Jenna, I think we need to talk. I know who the girl is and no, she is not my girlfriend. She is my ex-wife. If I would have seen her anywhere near the place, I would have followed you to the restroom. We have been divorced for over a year now. She has no right to do what she did tonight. I don't love her and if she would have loved me she would not have slept with Noah. She told me she was in love with him. I told you about this. I am not sure what she's trying to do here."

She keeps her eyes on the water. My guess is she is trying to process what I just told her. I wait for her to reply. Taking off my boots and rolling up my pants, I sit beside her and put my feet in the water. "Ethan is right, I don't do girlfriends. I told you that. When I caught her, I divorced her and I swore I would never let any girl into my heart again. I don't want to feel that pain ever again. That was before when

I thought there was no woman out there for me. That was before I laid eyes on you."

Still she won't look at me, so I take her by the chin to look at me. "Jenna, you don't have to leave. One call to her, and I promise she will never come within two hundred yards from you again. She will never hurt you or the baby, I promise. Please, give me a chance to show you that you are safe here. My mom would be crushed if you leave now, Jenna. Please don't go." I will do whatever it takes to keep her here.

"I only have a few weeks until I turn eighteen and go back home. Your mom has been like a mother to me. I feel safe here with her. I went through hell in the foster home before here. I had to worry day and night about if and when one of them drunks would walk into my room and beat me or harm my baby. I can't live like that again, and I won't."

Her tears are like bullets to my heart. What can I do or say? How do I keep her here? Mom. I need to get Mom here to talk to her. She will know what to do. I tell her I am going to get something to drink. I ask her if she wants anything. She says she is fine and will stay here until I get back.

Mom went to lay down earlier because she wasn't feel well. I hate to wake her, but I can't take the chance with Jenna wanting to leave. I have to wake her.

"Mom! Mom, can you please come talk to Jenna? She wants to leave Mom. You can't let her go!" She stares up at me from her sleepy eyes.

"What are you talking about leave? She was sleeping. What happened, Bryson? What time is it? What did you do?" What did I do? I would never do anything to make her run.

"It's only eight, mom. You haven't been sleeping long and I am sorry I had to wake you. I didn't do anything. Please, Mom. She's outside. Let's go now."

Mom gets out of bed and we go down to the pool. Mom calls out to Jenna, and she turns to look at Mom with tears rolling down her face. I stay back so Mom can talk to her. I sure hope she can stop her from leaving. Lord, what have you done to me? Please, don't dangle her in my face, and then take her away from me. I promise, I will make her and her child happy until the day I die.

While Mom and Jenna are talking, I take this time to go back to the barn. I pull out my phone and call Leah. I start cussing and telling her I will kill her if she comes anywhere near Jenna. She stops me by screaming in my ear.

"Bryson, I am in Baton Rouge, and I have no idea what you are talking about. Here, I will let you talk to Ryan, he can tell you where I am."

"Put him on the phone now." Ryan gets on the phone and I ask him. "Where has Leah, been tonight? If you fucking lie to me, I will rip your damn head off your shoulders."

"Bro, I swear we are in my apartment in Baton Rouge. I will Facetime you right now to prove it." I believe him, but who the fuck else could this be?

I hang up the phone and go back to where Mom and Jenna are talking. I sit by Jenna and tell her it was not Leah, but I will find out who it is. My mom is shocked. "Then who can it be Bry? You never dated anyone else besides Leah." I am going crazy trying to think who it can be.

"Please, Jenna, stay here, where we can protect you? Please don't leave, we will go crazy. I will get some of the ranch hands to watch the house at night. I will follow you to restrooms from now on so you are never alone. Please say you will stay?"

Please God, I promise to do whatever you want me to do. I will go to every Sunday mass and help homeless people on the side of the road. Please don't take her from me please.

"Okay I will stay, but we have to be more careful. We can't let people see us as a couple. I am not only worried for me and the baby, but I am worried about you and your family." Mom and I both hug her, and let her know we will get to the bottom of this and she we be safe.

Jenna and I go to the kitchen because I want her to eat something. "I don't know how to cook much, but I can try to make something for you to eat." She smiles her little dimple smile, and I melt.

"How about I cook for us? I am pretty good in the kitchen." Hot damn, beautiful and can cook. What more could a man ask for?

"Sure, do I need to run to the store, or do you think we can find something here?"

"I think we can find something here. Let's go raid the freezer and see what you like." Boy, she has no idea that I can eat just about anything. I follow her to the freezer which Mom keeps stocked. "Do you like crawfish etouffee?" Is she for real right now? Is it possible she can cook this?

"Hell, yeah! I eat just about anything, and if you're cooking it I know I will eat it." She laughs and shakes her head.

"Etouffee is quick and easy. Come on, I will let you help me." She doesn't have to tell me twice.

"Little darling I will follow you anywhere, just lead the way."

Before you know it we are moving around the kitchen like we were born to do this. She says what she needs and I get it. It sure smells good, and I hear my father coming into the kitchen. "Hey, good looking, what you got cooking? It sure smells damn good in here." My dad is just like me. You cook it, and we will definitely eat it.

"Hey, Dad. What are you doing?" He just gives me this blank look.

"I was doing some work in the office for a new client" We talk a bit more and I offer to help if I can.

Jenna tells me, "Bryson set the table. It's almost ready." I set four seats, not sure if mom will eat this or not. I grab the tea from the fridge, and put it on the table. Mom comes in just as we are about to sit. "Jenna it sure smells good." I see that little blush pop out on her cheeks.

"Thank you, I hope I don't disappoint you all. It's just an old recipe my grandmother passed down."

Dad sits down at the table and says, "Kristi had one of her migraines tonight so I ate a sandwich, but I think that will hit the spot. I was actually on my way to find some junk food to hold me over until breakfast. I will definitely pass on the junk for some ettouffee." Dad says grace and we dig in.

Oh my God, if I wasn't in love with this girl before, I would definitely be now. This food is so fricken amazing. "Oh, dear baby Jesus, this taste just like my Grandma Melba's etouffee. Where on earth did you learn to cook like this? Jenna's face turns red.

"My mother always insisted that I learn to cook. She passed down all my grandmother's Cajun recipes to me."

"So, are you telling me you can cook gumbo like the Cajuns?"

"I can cook that with my eyes closed."

"Mom, you know I love you, and I love the way you cook, but can she please cook a few days a week? You will love the way the Cajuns cook ,I promise."

My mom winks at Jenna and says, "Sure, I could use a break from the kitchen, and maybe I can follow your dad around like he wants and not have to worry about getting dinner on the table."

"What do you think Dad, should we keep her?"

John doesn't stop eating when he says, "She can cook, son. I haven't eaten etouffee like this since your grandma passed away. Not that your mom can't cook, because you know I love her cooking, but you are right. The Cajuns sure can cook." I smile so proud of my baby.

"Now, if I can get her to ride a horse beside me, I will have the perfect woman, besides you, Mom." Jenna is now all kinds of red.

"Thank you, Jenna. Everything was delicious. I will get everything clean so you can go get you some rest. You have had a long day."

"I will help you with the dishes, Mom."

"Oh, Bry. Get out of my kitchen. I will be fine. I give her a kiss on the cheek and tell her goodnight, before taking my girl up to her room.

"Thank you, baby, for everything we did together today. I want to share all my days and nights with you. This is just the beginning of a long life together." I kiss her and give a slap on the butt. She whips around and gives me that look. I can't help but laugh as I close the door and go to my room.

Chapter 16

Jenna

Bryson wants to go on a picnic at park he says is just down the road from the ranch. I am up for anything, as long as he is part of it. His mom and I pack up a lot more food than the two of us could possibly eat. She says, "With Bryson, you can never have enough food." I believe her. I have watched that man eat. I wonder where he puts it.

I am trying to get my hair up in a ponytail and come to the conclusion, I really must see about getting a haircut soon. I hear Bryson calling my name, asking if I am ready yet. I open my door, and watch the smile creep up on his face. I know this man will love me forever. What I don't understand is why? Why me?

We pull up at the park and Bryson jumps out. Something is up with him, I just know it. He has been smiling since he walked out of his room this morning. He runs around to my side, picks me up, and slowly puts me down, kissing my head. I stare up at him and wonder what he has up his sleeve. He opens the back door and hands me the blanket. He picks up the picnic basket and ice chest. We make our way under a beautiful old oak tree, and Bryson sets everything down. I spread the blanket out and we both sit. He still has that smile, I can't put my finger on it but, I know something is up.

With his back against the tree, I sit between his legs with my back against his chest. "Jenna can you tell me more about Caden?" It surprises me that he brings it up. While I was getting dressed I remembered how I had planned to take Caden on a picnic.

"He is the sweetest little boy you could ever meet. He never had much, and never asked for anything. My first night in that house, that little boy took a beating from a drunk to save me and my baby from getting hit."

"And I would do it again, rich girl."

I shoot to my feet, and there stands Caden and Bryan. I throw my arms around Caden and cry. "Oh, my God! I thought I would never see you again! Are you okay? Have they hurt you? Are you eating?" I never want to let him go. I want to take him so far away from all of this.

"I can't answer all the questions if I can't breathe, Jenna." I let him go and just look him over to see if he has any marks on him.

"I am doing fine. Since that night at the hospital, Bryan stood up for me. He told them if they touched me again, he would take me to the cops and they would go to jail. I really missed you. I prayed like you told me. I asked God to let me see you again, and he heard my prayers to see you. I only have one other prayer, and that is to see my sisters, Gaby and Jazzy, one day."

By this time, the tears are pouring down my face. Bryson just rubs my back. "Thank you, Bryan, for doing this for her. She really has missed him, but was afraid to contact anyone."

Bryson shakes Bryan's hand. I can't believe they are really here. We all sit down, and I ask Caden how he is doing on the game I left him, and if he can beat Bryan yet. "Bryan sucks. I beat him at everything, so he quits, but I just laugh at him." It's so good to see him smile.

I hear Kristi and we all turn. She is standing there with a woman and two little girls. Out of nowhere Caden runs and grabs the two girls. I walk up behind him and he looks up at me.

"Jenna, you make all my prayers come true! This is Gaby and this is Jazzy, my sisters. I love you so much for this, Jenna. Thank you, Jenna. Thank you so much. I can't believe this. I miss them so much."

I look up at Kristi and she puts her finger over her lips, and shushes me. I hug her and whisper 'how'. She says we will talk later. Caden checks out his sisters the way I checked over him to make sure there are no marks or bruises. Kristi introduces Bryson and I to Taren. Taren is the foster mother of Gaby and Jazzy, and she lives here in Beaumont. The three of them sit on the ground and talk. Kristi, Taren, and I all walk back over to the men and watch from afar. The sight of those three babies together, has filled my heart to the rim. Bryson pulls me in for a hug, and asks if I am alright. I nod my head because there is no way I can talk with my heart in my throat. He kisses my head and whispers, "This is only the beginning, my love. I will make all your dreams come true." I shut my eyes and thank God and all his angels for sending me this man, just when I needed him most.

Once we are home, Bryson carries me up to my room. I tell him my feet hurt, and he looks down and freaks out. He screams down for his mom to hurry and come to my room. When she gets to the room, she has the most horrifying look on her face. Bryson makes her look at my feet and she says that's normal for a pregnant woman. They have a little spat because he scared her so bad, and he sends me off to the shower, promising me a night of rest and relaxation in his bed with a movie. Life is good, too good.

Logan, my lawyer, has drawn up the paperwork for Justin to sign over his rights to the baby. I gave him Justin's phone number, so he will contact Justin to come in and sign them sometime this week. He will let me know when everything is done. It's really nice to have friends in high places. My father and I did a survey job for Logan when I was down for Christmas, so he refuses to take payment for the paperwork. I will be happy when it's all over with. Today is Jenna's surprise, and I can't wait to see her face. Mom has packed us a picnic lunch. Jenna thinks we are just going to go relax and have a picnic.

"Jenna, are you ready to go?" She steps out of her room with her hair pulled up in a pony tail and a cute little yellow sundress that hugs her baby bump.

"Bryson, it's a picnic. Can you please stop rushing me?" That girl, she can't leave this house without every hair in place, and every wrinkle out of her clothes. How did I get so lucky?

Seeing my girl cry with happiness is worth everything in the world to me. After all the stress Jenna has been through the past few weeks, I wanted to do something to bring joy back to her life. Watching her face when she heard Caden's voice was priceless. I would do whatever I could to see this much happiness on her face every day.

Bryan and Mom showing up with the girls, and seeing Caden made Jenna's face light up like it was Christmas morning. I knew what my mom and I had put together was right in every sense. I can't even imagine going through a fourth of what these children have been through. I just hope this gives them the strength to hold on until they can be back together again.

Grabbing a football from the truck I ask, "Hey! Caden and Bryan, you guys want to throw around the football?" They both agreed but I could tell Caden was a little hesitant to leave his sisters.

Jenna steps up, "Go ahead and play football Caden, I will take the girls to swing and slide for a while. I promise you they will be fine." Caden was ok with that and explained to his sisters.

"Jenna is my guardian angel and she will take good care of you. I will be right here playing football if you need me okay?" The girls say okay and go off with Jenna. The whole day was amazing and watching Jenna forget all her troubles, is worth the world to me. I going to hard to top this one. I don't think we could knock the smile off her face with a chisel and hammer.

Bryan, Caden, and I are throwing the ball around when I hear the ice cream truck coming down the road.

"Jenna, bring the girls over here, the ice cream truck is coming." I watch as she grabs the girl's hands and heads my way. Most people want to turn back time, but not me I want the next few weeks to fly. I want to make this woman all mine. She is beautiful, smart, loving, caring, and the strongest person I know. I don't think I could have gotten through the death of my parents like she did. Much less being put into a horrible home, where she always had to be on alert. She was not only scared for her life but for Caden, and the life of her unborn child. Geez, I swear I will make all of that up to her any way I can.

"Hey, Gaby, what kind of ice cream do you want?"

"I'm not Gaby, I'm Jazzy."

I laugh and say, "Okay, Jazzy, what would you like?" Both girls chose what ice cream they want. "What kind do you want Caden?"

"I don't want anything, thank you."

"Are you sure, Buddy?"

"Yes. You have done enough for me already."

"I didn't ask if you needed ice cream, I asked what you wanted, Caden. Pick something you want and I mean it."

Caden smiles and looks up at me. "If you're sure, I will take a Push up." After I order for myself and Jenna, and everyone has what they need, we head over to the blanket to enjoy the cold treats, and visit with the children. My Jenna will make one hell of a mother. She is so tentative with the girls, but at the same time she is listening to Caden rattle on about his video games.

Taren says she hates to break up the party but she has to get home and get dinner ready. Jenna's smile slowly fades. I pull her to me and whisper in her ear.

"Taren is one of my mom's friends, we can see the girls any time you want." She looks over her shoulder at me.

"Really baby? Are you serious?" I give her a nod and a wink and her amazing smile is back. We hug the girl's good bye and walk them to the van to help get the buckled up. Caden promises to call them, and Taren says he can see them anytime he wants, she just needs a day's notice.

We wave to Gaby and Jazzy as they pull away. Caden comes and hugs Jenna. "Jen, I don't know what I would do if I hadn't met you. You did more for me than anyone. I just need one more favor from you, and I will never ask for another thing again." I stay close to make sure if Jenna can't do the favor than maybe I can.

"Sure, honey, anything. You know I will do what I can." He lifts his chin and stands taller like he has to pump himself up.

"Can I still be there when you have the baby, like we planned before you left me?" My Jenna's face lights up. You can see how much she loves this kid.

"Oh honey, of course you can be there. I will make sure someone calls Bryan on my way to the hospital, and he can get you there. And I need you to know, I didn't leave you because I wanted to. Kathie came and took me away. I didn't have a choice, just like you don't have a choice to go where you want to go. I think about you every day, and I pray that God would keep you safe. Please, don't ever think I left you because I wanted to."

"So, why didn't you come for me? I prayed every day that you would come for me but you didn't. Why?" I wrap my arm around Caden.

"Hey, Buddy. Jenna wanted to go for you, but she couldn't. The state would never allow her to take you. She couldn't tell anyone about what happens in that house either, you may have been moved where we couldn't find you. I took a big chance getting in contact with Bryan to set this up. So

"So you see buddy, we can't really go against social services or we could all be in trouble, and right now Jenna doesn't need any trouble okay?"

He seems to understand, so we make our way to Bryan's car so we can see them off. Giving Caden a big hug, Jenna says, "I love you Caden and I always will. Please remember that, this is not goodbye, it's just see ya later. Okay?" He gives her a big hug.

"I love you too Jenna. See ya later, gator." He smiles and jumps in Bryan's car and they drive away. Jenna turns towards me, buries her face in my chest and cries. I just let her cry and get it all out.

"Baby we can see Caden when you want, okay? We know he is not being abused anymore. Please, don't get so upset, it's not good for the baby."

What she doesn't know is that I got him a cell phone and programmed our numbers in it, so he can call us anytime. I decided not to tell her because I know it will be an awesome surprise when she hears his voice over the phone for the first time. Bryan promised he would show Caden how to use it, and explain to him that he can't call her and upset her, but if he needs to vent he can call me. I don't need her stressed out.

Jenny is very tired when we get home, so I pick her up and carry her up to her room. "A nice warm shower will make you feel better. I will go down and get us a movie and we can lie on my bed and be lazy. Okay?" I can never do enough for this woman. I love her so much. Her smiles just brightens my day

"That sounds good to me, my feet hurt." I look down and her feet are swollen and I freak out. I scream down for my mom to get up here. She runs into the room and I show her Jenna's feet.

"Bryson Erin Alexander, if you ever scream at me again like someone is dying, I am going to beat on your head with a damn broom. She is pregnant and her feet will swell, son. Geez, you almost gave me a heart attack." I didn't mean to scare her. I just didn't know what to do. I knew it wasn't normal.

"Well, after her shower she is going to lie down and put her feet up, and we will call the doctor tomorrow." I wonder if the doctor can give her something. There has to be a pill.

"Putting her feet up is good, but calling the doctor is useless, but if it makes you feel better, then be my guest. She has been on her feet since 5:00 am and the seafood we ate had a lot of salt. So we need to watch her salt intake."

Bullshit, we will take her off salt and I will carry her everywhere she needs to go if I have to. "Sorry I scared you mom but I shit when I saw her feet so swollen." She shakes her head and leaves the room. I turn to Jenna so I can carry her to the bathroom. "Please, be quick in the shower so I can get your feet up." I kiss her head, and walk her to the shower before going to my room.

Chapter 17

Things go smoothly for the next couple of weeks. Ethan and Ramie went back to Baton Rouge without me. They were a little upset that I stayed behind, but Ramie and I had a long talk. I told her I had found my forever. She says it's nice to see me finally happy, and she still says I was never in love with Leah. I think she's right because what I felt for Leah is nothing close to what I feel for Jenna. I really believe I was trying to make things happen with Leah because I wanted the perfectly planned out life.

There is one thing that I have learned over the years. If you want to make God laugh, make plans. He always seems to have his own plan. I never thought I would fall in love again, and look at me now. I haven't even thought of another girl since I laid eyes on my Jenna. Today, I am sneaking off to buy something pink for my little princess with the money I won from the bet. Mom says to make sure I pick up a baby book, so Jenna can start writing in it. Dad says to find pink cowboy boots, but I don't think they come that small. There will be time later for me to make her daddy's little cowgirl. First, I have to get her mother on a horse.

I go up to Jenna's room to let her know that I am going to run some errands and ask if she needs anything in town, but she is sound asleep. I kiss her and leave her sleeping. Mom is in the kitchen when I come through. She asks if we could have a talk before I go. I have been waiting for this but I can't say I am ready.

"I need to know what's going on in that head of yours, Bryson." I knew this was what she wanted to know.

"What do you mean by that, Mom?" Playing dumb with Mom is not a good idea, but I try it anyway.

"I know you and Jenna have become pretty close since you came home, but I need to know how close. Where are you going with this?" Well, I would just as soon tell her everything and let her chew my ass out, and get this over with.

"I love her, Mom." Her eyes go wide, and I think they are going to pop out of her head at any minute.

"YOU WHAT? You have only known her a couple of months, son! Jenna is only seventeen, Bry. You could get into a lot of trouble." Who cares? People fall in love at first sight every day. When your heart knows what it wants, who cares about the timing?

"I loved her the minute I saw her at the top of the stairs. She took my breath away at that very moment, and I still haven't gotten it back. We have done nothing wrong that would get me in trouble, Mom. I am not stupid, and I will not touch her until she is eighteen."

"Bry, you do understand, that she is keeping this baby and that means it's a package deal right?" Does she think I don't know this? That we haven't talked about it?

"Yes ma'am, I do. I wouldn't have it any other way. The jackass that got her pregnant has already signed over his rights. I want to give the baby my name if Jenna allows it. I saw her heartbeat, Mom. Do you know what that did to me? She moves every time I touch Jenna. She knows my voice. I want her and Jenna to be mine. When I married Leah, I thought it was love, but love had nothing to do with it. I wanted what you and Dad have. The love that nothing and no one could ever come between. Leah was not my forever, and I know that now, because I never loved Leah like I love Jenna."

"Have you two… you know, done it?" I can't believe she even thinks this way of me.

"Of course not ,Mom, she is only seventeen and I will not touch her like that. That's what I am trying to tell you. We haven't had sex, nor have we talked about it. I. Love. Her. I love everything about her, the way she smiles. Her laugh. Her strength. Her courage. And her heart. Jenna is everything, all rolled into one, Mom. She is going to be the best mother and wife. You know you saw it too, at the park with those kids. She has so much love and motherly instincts. I am just in awe of her, and it happens more and more each day."

"Okay, one more question, and I will stop drilling you. What are you going to do when it's time to go back for your last semester?" Here goes the hard part. I know I am in trouble with this one but she has to understand.

"I am not sure if I will go back this semester. She needs me here, and I plan on being here for her." I will not back down. I can only pray she understands how strongly I feel about the decisions I will make.

"Bryson Erin Alexander, you cannot throw away four years of college, son. I will take care of her while you're gone, but I will not let you quit now." My dad walks in about this time, and Lord knows, I am thankful.

"I am not quitting, Mom. I will either sit this semester out and go back after she has the baby, or I will finish it off at a local college. I am not throwing it away." She turns to my father for him to back her up.

"John, help me out here. We cannot let him do this, can we?" My dad and I have talked about this. He understands me. He has even given me his blessing.

"Kristi, he is a grown man in love. Do you think my mother and father could have talked me out of being with you for the birth of our child?" My dad is all about family. That's where I get it from, I guess.

"That's just it John, it's not his child."

That's it. I won't let her say that again. This baby is my child, and if she can't handle that, I am taking Jenna and we are out of here today. I slap the counter. "But it is my child. She will always be my child. I will love her just as you love me. Have you not heard one word I have said, Mom? I love them both and Jenna gave me the father's rights. I hope to God you take the same rights as grandparents, too. But I never want to hear you say that baby is not mine, again."

"Calm down son, do not use that tone with your mother. I don't think your mother means it that way at all. Kristi, Bryson and I had this discussion in the barn a couple of days ago. If he feels he needs to sit out a semester, then so be it. Four months more won't hurt us. He has promised to finish and I believe him. I have also told him I can't wait for my first grandbaby to be here."

Mom turns to me and tears come to both of our eyes. "I love her Mom, I really do and I can't wait to meet our baby girl. Please be with me and not against me. I have kept my hands off of her because I want everything to be done right. You taught me how to be a man, and if I ever needed you more in my life, it's now." The tears roll down her face. I hope that means she sees things my way.

"Oh Bry, I'm sorry. I didn't mean it that way, and yes, I am on your side and I can't wait to hold my granddaughter."

Thank you, Jesus. I couldn't see my life without my parents in it. But I will always stand up for Jenna and our baby. "I love you Mom. Thank you and I give you my word, I will only sit out one semester and I will finish my degree." I assure her I am not throwing it all away. Jenna needs me and I will be here.

"I know you will,honey, and I am so proud of you." I have the best parents, and I hope they know how much I love and respect them.

"Jenna is sleeping, so I am going to hurry out to see what I can buy our little princess." I want to be the first one to buy her something. I think it will lift Jenna's spirits some too.

"Oh, Bryson, can I come with you please? I would like to pick out a few things myself." Oh geez mom and shopping is not my favorite but I won't refuse her.

"Sure, Mom let's go."

Now I know why I don't take my mom shopping anymore. Geez, this woman has to look and touch everything. Her hands are full of pink this and pink that. It looks like she spilled a bottle of Pepto. This baby girl will be so spoiled. "Come on, Mom, we need to go, Jenna will be waking up soon." She gives me a sad face but then she sees it's not working on me.

"Okay, okay. You are just like your father. Always in a hurry."

I shake my head and make my way to the check out. I pay for the things I have bought and, of course, the money I won didn't come close to being enough. Like I said, my princess will never want or need for anything. Mom finally checks out and we haul it all to my truck. Mom and I have a little small talk on how the neighbors are doing and who is running around on whom. Mom is not one for gossip but she sure knows what's happening within a fifty mile radius.

Chapter 18

Jenna

I awake to the door bell constantly ringing. I get up and go down stairs but I don't see anyone in the house. If I had to guess, they are all at the barn. I open the door, and I am slapped across the face.

"Bitch, I warned you. Pack your shit, and get the hell out of here. If I catch you around him again, you won't live to talk about it. Now, this is your last warning. He loves me. Look at you, you are a pathetic loser who can't even keep her legs closed. Just because you're pregnant doesn't mean he will stay with you. He will never love you like he loves me."

"Who are you? Are you Leah?" She laughs the weirdest laugh I have ever heard.

"Leah? That bitch couldn't hold on to him either. Give her a little meth and she was sleeping with everyone but him. I am leaving and you have exactly two hours to be gone, or I will be back for you." I slam and lock the door. I run to my room and lock the door there too. I begin packing and text Angel to come get me. I tell her that something bad has happened, and I need her here now.

Angel asks for the address and tells me she's on her way. I pack all I can and wait. I have to leave Kristi a note. I have to tell her I am safe. She deserves to know that I am going someplace where my baby and I will be okay. I can't believe everything Bryson told me was a lie. Lies. Just like Justin. I am just happy I didn't give him all of me. I pace the floor, waiting for Angel to get there.

As Angel pulls up, I race to her car with my bags. "Hurry, Angel. We have to go. Hurry!" I am trying to load my suitcases into the car as fast as possible.

Angel gets out of the car to help me load my bags, and ask, "What in the hell is going on, Jenna? Why is your face swollen? Who did this to you?" We can talk about it in the car, but first she needs to help me so we can leave quickly.

"I will tell you later, but we have to go, NOW!" Finally she loads my bags and we head out. I keep watching behind us to see if we are being followed. I don't see anything suspicious, but that doesn't mean it's not possible. I am so scared, and so pissed at Bryson. How could he do this? He promised me there was no other person besides his ex-wife, Leah. He lied to me.

"Start talking, Jenna, or I am going to pull this car over." How do I know she is serious? Because, she once pulled over four lanes and stopped just to chew my ass out for not telling her I was dating Zach. Everyone was after him because he was the quarterback. I didn't know if things would last, so I didn't tell anyone as to save myself the embarrassment.

"Oh, Angel. I don't even know where to start." How much do I want to tell her? She is going to go all Hulk on this shit.

"Try the beginning, Jenna. I need to know what has you like this. I thought you told me they were good people and you loved it there? Who hit you?" Oh my God, she thinks the Alexander's hit me. Kristi and John couldn't hurt a flea.

"They are good people, and they would never hurt me. See, they have a son that came home from college about a month or so ago. He has been super sweet and overly protective of me and the baby."

"So? He hit you?" Yeah like that would happen.

"No, he would never hit me. He was married before, and got a divorce. He and I went to the movies a couple of weeks ago. I went to the restroom and this girl cornered me and told me I better stay away from him. I told him about it and he thought it was his ex. He called her and threatened her. She swore it wasn't her and she even had people that vouched for her that she was still in Baton Rouge and had never left."

"Ok, so who hit you?" I might as well start from the beginning.

"I was sleeping and the doorbell kept ringing, so I got up to answer the door, and when I did she slapped me. She told me this was my last warning. I only had two hours to get away from here. I should never come back, or she would kill me." I wait for reply.

"She said she would kill you?" Not in those exact words, but it's what she meant.

"Well, she said she would be back and I would not live to tell anyone about it. To me, this would mean kill."

"Do you know who she is, Jenna?" I wish I knew her name, so that Bryson could make sure she stops.

"No, I don't, and Bryson swears he never loved or dated anyone other than his ex-wife, Leah, and his mother confirmed that."

At the moment, my phone starts ringing. I check to see who is calling, and it's Bryson. I can't answer it. I push ignore. He calls again and again, so I put it on silent. "Who is that calling?" Angel asks me.

"Bryson!" I know the questions are coming, and I try to prepare myself.

"Why don't you answer him, Jenna?"

"I don't want him to know where I am going." If he knows where I am, he will come for me. I don't need him or his lies.

"Where are you going, Jenna? I can't take you to my house and you can't go to yours. What are you going to do, call Miss Fancy Pants?"

Oh my God, I didn't think about that. What am I going to do? If I call Kathie she will put me in a new home. I can't do another home. "Just take me to my house. I will hide out there until I figure something out." I will get in my car and drive to Mexico if necessary.

"What if this crazy bitch knows where you live? You can't stay there alone, Jenna. You have to come up with something else." She's right, but I know where Dad keeps his gun, and I have a very good aim.

"I will lock myself inside and set the alarm. Angel, please take me home." We fall silent and my phone keeps vibrating. Now Kristi is calling. What have I done? She must be so worried about me. I will just call her later to let her know, I am alright.

Angel drops me off at my house and helps me to take my bags inside. "Lock up and set the alarm, Jenna. I have to go to work but I will stop by afterwards and check on you ok?"

"Yes. Thank you, Angel, and I love you."

"I love you too. Text me, if you need me and if she comes around here, call 911. You hear me?"

"I will, I promise." Angel leaves and I go to the bathroom to get me a cold rag to put on my face. Her hand print is still there. I can't believe she hit me.

I sit on the toilet and cry. After a while I get up, and go to the living room to lie down on the couch. I whisper to myself, "Why Lord? Why would you give me the best home, with wonderful people, and then take it away from me? What have I done, now? Why? Please tell me why?" My phone goes off again, and it's Bryson. Against my better judgement, I answer it. "Hello?"

"Jenna? Where are you, baby?" He gave up that right when he lied to me.

"Don't call me that, and you don't need to know. Just leave me alone." I don't need another liar. I don't need anyone.

"Jenna, what is going on? I need to know where you are, please?"

"I am safe and that's all you need to know. Tell your parents I am sorry and thanks for everything they did for me." I am angry and hurt.

"No, Jenna, I won't tell them anything. I need to see you. Please tell me where you are, now." I start to cry and I can't form words. "Jenna, what happened? Baby, where are you? Are you and the baby okay? Please, tell me Jenna, please." He's crying and it breaks my heart in two.

"Home. I'm home." I tell him softly.

"No you're not home. My dad saw you get into a blue car with a girl, and leave. Please, tell me where?" I forgot his home is considered my home until I am eighteen.

"My parents' home, in Houston, Bryson." I hear him let out a pinned up breath.

"I figured that. I am only three miles away. I will be there soon, but I want you to stay on the phone with me okay?" Thank God because I am scared. I feel so lost and alone

."Yes please hurry, I am so scared." Everything seems so overwhelming I hope and pray Bryson is careful. But I want him to hurry regardless.

"Scared of what, my love? Is someone there with you?"

"No, I am alone now." Alone, and so scared!

"Tell me what you're scared of baby? Did I do something wrong?" I can't believe Bryson thinks it's something he did.

"No, I don't know." I hear his truck in the driveway.

"Baby, I am in the driveway. Go open the door." I jump off the couch and go to the door.

"Okay." I hang up the phone, and wait, at the front door to see Bryson through the peep hole. When he appears, I open the door. He throws his arms around me and picks me up. He brings me to the couch, and he sits me on his lap.

"What happened baby, why did you run?" I look at him, and he freaks out. "WHO THE FUCK HIT YOU, JENNA?" I wish I could give him a name but she never told me.

"It was her Bryson. I opened the door and she slapped me. She said I only had two hours to get out of your house or she was coming back to kill me." I have never in my life been so scared. I think I was more afraid she would hurt my baby.

"Who is she, baby? What are you telling me?" I calm down so he doesn't blow up.

"The girl from the movies, she says you love her. I asked if she was Leah, and she said no, and that you didn't love Leah like you love her." He pulls out his phone to make a call.

"Who are you calling, Bryson?"

"I am calling Ethan, just to make sure it's not Leah. I trust Ethan more than I do Ryan. If Ethan says she is in Baton Rouge, than I will scratch her from the list."

He dials the phone and puts it on speaker. "Ethan, are you in Baton Rouge?" Ethan answers quickly.

"Yea, man, what's up?"

"Have you seen Leah?"

"Actually I just dropped her off at Ryan's about thirty minutes ago after my meeting why?" Why would he be with Bryson's ex? This is weird.

"Are you sure? Don't fucking lie to me, Ethan." I wonder if he is upset because they were together. He says it's been over and he has no feelings for her.

"Bryson, dude, I have no reason to lie to you. What the fuck is up with you?" Bryson is getting so upset because he can't figure it out. He takes a deep breath before he speaks.

"Some bitch slapped my girl today, and I need to find out who it is. She told Jenna I am in love with her. I can't figure out who that would be. I never even dated anyone else. Dude, help me here."

"Dude, I have no Idea, I know you never dated anyone but her. This shit is fucked up. Is there anything I can do?" I wish he was here but I won't tell him that.

"I will let you know. I may need you to come back and help me if I can't get to the bottom of this shit soon." I sure hope it's soon.

"I'm just a phone call away bro. You know that." I see now what a great friendship they have. Ethan is like Angel always there when needed.

"Thanks, bro. Later."

"Later, dude." He hangs up the phone, and I hear a car pull up and I grab his arm.

"It's ok baby. It's only, Mom and Dad. They were out looking for you too. I sent them a text when I was on the phone with you." I relax, and he puts me down to go let them in. Kristi runs to me to see if I am okay.

"Jesus, Jenna! What happened?" Before I can say anything Bryson speaks up.

"Sit down Mom. I will explain everything, and then we need to figure out what to do." Bryson explains everything and his dad says we have to go back to Beaumont and file a police report. I am scared shitless, and not too sure I want to go back.

"Bryson, I can't go back there. She will come for me and kill me next time. I can't take that chance." He has to understand how scared I am.

"Baby, listen to me please. I only left today because Dad was in the barn, and I thought you would sleep until I got back. I promise, I will not leave your side again until this psycho woman is caught and behind bars. I will sleep on the floor, next to your bed if that's what it takes, but I will not leave here without you."

I know he would never let anyone hurt me. "Okay,, Bryson I will go back, but you have to promise to take me with you. At least wake me up before you leave so I know I am alone."

"I promise baby, I will do whatever it takes."

"Okay, I have to get something from the office. I will be right back." I open the safe and take out some more money, just in case I need it. I also unlock his top drawer pulling out his gun. I am looking for the clip when Bryson walks in.

"Why do you have that gun, Jenna? Do you even know how to use a gun?" I am caught red handed so there is no way to deny it.

"Yes, my dad and I used to go to the range and shoot a couple times a month. He wanted to make sure I was safe when he was away on business."

"But you will be safe with me. You don't need that. Let's leave it here and let the cops handle this, please? I don't want you around guns right now. Too many accidents happen with guns. Besides dad and I have guns we hunt with at home."

"Okay." I agree and lock the gun up. He smiles and picks me up. "You shouldn't be on your feet young lady." I giggle when he bites my neck and he carries me back to the living room, where John and Kristi are pacing.

John is on the phone and turns to ask, "Bryson were you followed here?"

"I don't know Dad, I was too busy with driving and trying to get Jenna to answer my calls. I didn't really pay attention." Shit I can't believe I didn't think of that.

"Well let's play this on the safe side. We will turn the outside lights off. You will carry your mom to the truck and leave. Jenna and I will hang back for a few minutes to see if you are followed, then we will get in moms car and leave."

Bryson shakes his head, "No way dad, I will not letting Jenna out of my sight again. If you are worried then you give me your hat and you carry mom out to my truck. We are pretty much the same build so they can't tell us apart in the dark." John agrees. Bryson loads my suitcases and John carries Kristi out to Bryson's truck and they leave. Bryson picks me up and carries me to the kitchen and puts me on the bar. "So this is your house, huh?"

"Yup, all mine. I am not sure if I can stay here until this is over, but it's paid for. Well, actually everything is paid for."

"Are you serious? Your dad must have made some major money."

"Yes, and it helped that my mom managed money really well, too. Not to mention my dad sold his business like six months before the accident."

"Can I see your bedroom?" I laugh and try to remember what it looked like when I left here. I don't guess it matters.

"Sure. if you want to." Bryson helps me down and I lead him to my bedroom. He goes in and looks around at the pictures of me in my cheerleading uniform. He turns and looks at me.

"You're a cheerleader, huh?" Those days are over now, but I won't let that get me down.

"Was, actually I was captain, but I'm sure that once they find out about the baby, I will be kicked from the team." He looks at me and gives me that sexy look.

"But you will always be my sexy ass cheerleader, baby." He gives me that wink I have come to love so much.

"I think we need to leave before we get in trouble." He laughs and grabs the picture. We head down and set the alarm before we lock up and leave in his mom's SUV. He calls

John to make sure everything is clear. John says no one followed them, but to make sure we don't have anyone on our tail. John has also contacted the Beaumont police, and they will be getting there to make a report.

As we are driving home I turn to look at Bryson's profile. He is so handsome. "Baby, you sure look different driving an SUV. I am so used to you always driving your truck." He looks over at me and smiles.

"My love, if I keep you barefoot and pregnant like I plan on doing, we are going to need an SUV." I'm not sure if I am happy or scared of that comment, so I smile at him.

"Twelve is my limit." Now let's see his reaction to that one.

"Yeah buddy. You spit them out, and I'll keep planting them." Damn this man! I never get to win with him. But, after being an only child, I never want that for my child. The more the merrier.

"Bring it, cowboy!"

We make it back to Beaumont without anyone following us. Bryson carries me into the house, and places me on the couch. Kristi is quickly at my side to make sure the swelling on my face is going down.

"Jenna, did she hit you anywhere else? Do you think you need to see your doctor?" She only hurt my heart by making me doubt Bryson, but I keep that to myself.

"No, ma'am. She only slapped me in the face. I think I am fine, but I will let Dr. Lacy know when I see her." Bryson announces that the officers are here to get my statement. My mouth is dry and I am so scared. What happens if they don't catch her? I can't keep living in constant fear.

"Bryson, can I please have a bottled water?" He stops pacing and heads to the kitchen.

"Here, baby. Do you need anything else?" I shake my head in response. "After you give your statement, you're going to have to eat something, okay?"

"Yes, I will. My stomach has been growling since we left Houston." I am pregnant, and I should not let it get to this point, but my nerves would not have let me eat.

"Why didn't you tell me? We could have stopped along the way? Girl, if you don't start speaking up, I am going to put you over my knee."

What the hell does he mean? Put me over his knee for what? "Why would you do that?" John, Kristi and Bryson all look at each other and laugh, and boy, does that piss me off.

"Oh baby, that was only a joke. You know! 'Put you over my knee and spank your butt'." Oh. My. God! Did he mean it sexually, in front of his parents? Hell to the NO. He will get an ass-chewing when we get upstairs. That shit is not even funny.

"Are you Jenna Kingsley?" One of the officers ask.

"Yes sir, I am." I answer. He gives me a couple of sheets of paper with lines on it.

"I need you to write down everything that happened starting when you opened the door." I take the pages and begin to write it all down.

After the officer takes all the information I have, he tells us they will be looking for this person. They will also have some extra units patrolling around here for the next few days. John sees them out when they are finished. This helps me to relax some. Kristi calls us all to the table. Bryson tries to hold my hand, but I jerk it away. He steps in front of me, "Why did you pull away from me baby? What did I do?"

"You know what you did, now move so I can go eat."

"I don't know. Can you please tell me so I can fix it?" I stare into his beautiful eyes, but I won't back down.

"You can't fix this, now move." He puts his hand on my cheek and slowly rubs it.

"Baby, please don't do this. I have been through hell and back today and the last thing I need is you mad at me for God only knows what." I squint my eyes and harden my lips.

"You made a sexual comment in front of your parents. You're making me look stupid because I don't know much about sex. Now, are you happy? You still can't fix this, and I am hungry." He kisses my cheek and gives my neck a little bite.

"I can, and I will, after we eat." He winks and we move to the dining room. Damn him and that wink.

Eating dinner like it was his last meal, Bryson finishes before me and goes out to the barn. I finish up my food before I go out to meet him. We talk about what was said and he explains what he meant. He's so cute when he is worried about me being upset. I want to kiss him so bad, so I do. I can't even describe the feelings I get when this man is near me. People talk about how they get butterflies in their stomachs. Well, I think it's more like swans for me.

I am so excited to set up the things we bought, for the baby that I can't wait to wake Jenna up and surprise her. Mom said we can use the nursery she had set up years ago. She had all the old baby stuff removed, but the walls are still pink and white. I really didn't expect her to give that room up. Maybe this being her granddaughter, has changed her heart.

I quietly peek in to see if Jenna is still asleep. She's not in her bed. Shit. I check the bathroom and nothing is in there. I run downstairs and start calling her name. Nothing. The barn. I bet she went to see Butta and Bella. I trot out there and see if Dad has seen her.

"Have you seen Jenna?" He gives me a funny look.

"Yeah, she left about an hour ago with a girl." Left? Why didn't she call me? She doesn't know anyone here. Something isn't right here.

"Are you sure, Dad? What color car was it?" Hopefully he got a good description of the car.

"It was blue, that weird blue. A little sports car." I think I remember her saying Angel had a blue car. I run back to the house and grab my phone to call her. It rings twice and then goes to voicemail. I keep trying. Damn, she is ignoring me. Now I am worried.

I am startled when Mom screams for me to come here. Running quickly towards the kitchen and Mom's voice, I find her holding a letter and crying. "Mom what is it?" All I can think of is a ransom letter.

"A letter from, Jenna. She's gone Bry. She said she has to go where she and the baby are safe. What does that mean, son? We kept her safe. Why would she leave?" I wish I knew the answer to her question

"I don't know, Mom, but I am going to find out. Dad said she left with a girl in a blue car. I think that's her friend from Houston. I will head that way."

Having followed me into the house, Dad asks "What do we do, son?" My brain is not working so I have to try hard to think about what we need to do.

"Ride into town and see, if you can spot them at one of the fast food places, or maybe the gas stations. They may have gone to get something to eat. I am going to Houston." My mom's face is so sad and I know that she is worried about Jenna, too.

"Son, please be careful and let me know as soon as you find her." My gut tells me that Jenna is in Houston because she doesn't know anyone around here. Jenna will go back to things and places that are familiar to her.

I run every stop sign and red light possible on the way to Houston. I have to get to her. I don't know why she thinks she has to find safety. What has happened to her? Is it Justin? Is it Leah? Could it possibly be a ranch hand? I am not sure but, I plan on finding out. I continue to call Jenna throughout the drive. I leave messages, begging for her to call me, or at least pick up the phone. The closer I get, the faster I go. Please, God. Let her be alright. I can't live without her.

Finally, Jenna answers the phone. "Hello?"

"Jenna. Where are you, baby?" Thank God she finally answered her phone.

"Don't call me that, and it's nothing you need to know. Just leave me alone." What the fuck? What did I do? Why is she talking to me this way? I try and calm her so she will talk to me. She is so cold to me, and my heart feels like it's going to explode in my chest. I get choked up and tears fall down my face.

"Please, tell me Jenna, please."

After an all too long pause, she finally tells me she is in Houston, just as I had figured. After I tell her I am almost there but not to hang up the phone, I shoot a text letting Mom know where she is.

"Jenna I'm at your front door. Let me in." As soon as she opens the door, I grab her quickly, and hug her tight. I sit her down on my lap as I sit on the couch.

"What happened, Jenna? Why did you run?" She turns to look at me, and believe me when I say, I was not prepared to see the marks on her face.

I lose my shit, "Who. The. Fuck. Hit. You!?"

She starts saying 'her' and 'she' and I am not following. She explains more and it's the girl that she ran into at the movies. My fucking blood is boiling and I am ready to kill. I pull out my phone and call Ethan. He tells me he dropped off Leah about thirty minutes ago in Baton Rouge. I want to ask why she was with him, but I really couldn't give two shits right now. I hang up just as Mom and Dad get here. Mom makes a beeline straight to Jenna. I explain to them what has happened. Now we try to plan our next move. To say I am angry would be an understatement. No one threatens my girl and baby and gets away with it. Someone will pay for this shit.

The trip back home to Beaumont was uneventful and no one followed us. Mom was preparing dinner, so Jenna and I sit in the living room until she was ready for us. I made a bad joke, and now Jenna is mad as shit at me. I really thought every girl her age would have read Fifty Shades. I would never touch her like that, well unless she begged me to, but I really don't think I could leave a mark on her.

"That was delicious Mom, thank you. Now I think it's time to get Jenna up to bed." Jenna gives me those mean eyes and I know my ass is going to pay. Jenna says she doesn't need my help getting her to bed. I decide to play her game. "Fine, then, I will just go to the barn and say goodnight to the other women in my life."

She shrugs her shoulders and says, "I am sure you can spank them and they would still love you." She gives me that, 'now what you going say cowboy,' look. I wink and leave the table.

After putting my plate in the sink, I walk out through the back door, and go straight to Butta. I start brushing her down, while Bella plays at my feet like always. I am making my way around to the other side, when I hear her voice.

"How could you say that in front of your parents? Now what are they going to think about me?"

I shake my head, "What do you think I meant by that, Jenna?" There she goes with the eyes again. Only this time, if they were bullets, I would be dead.

"You meant it in a sexual way and I didn't appreciate that in front of your parents." I throw back my head and start laughing.

"Woman, did you not read 50 Shades?" She looks at me so confused and shakes her head no.

"Angel and I talked about seeing the movie next year, but with school and cheerleading, I never had the time to read it. What does that book have to do with what you said?"

Now, I have to explain that I read the book. A book my friends would make fun of me about till the day I die. "In the book there is a rich guy who gets off on spanking girls. He likes it when they do wrong things, so he can take them to his special room and spank them. Now, I didn't mean it that way so hear me out. I would never get off to hurting you in any way. The girl he is falling in love with doesn't like to be spanked. So when she does something wrong, he tells her he is going to put her over his knee, and spank her. Because she doesn't like it, she learns to make better decisions. I didn't mean anything sexual by that remark, and if I could take it back, I would. I'm sorry, it was only a joke."

Her eyes soften as she closes the space between us. Jenna gets up on her tip toes to try to reach my lips, but she is still too short. So I lean my head down to meet her lips, and I kiss her. Not just a simple kiss, I mean a full-on kiss. She grabs behind my head, and I feel her tongue looking for entrance into my mouth. I open and give it to her, our tongues tangle together and I lift her up. She brings her legs to my hips, and I know I have to stop this now. Lord knows I don't want to, but my head is telling me we are too close to go and ruin it now. I slowly pull away from her, and rest my forehead on hers.

"Baby, I knew you would taste like Heaven, and I would love to haul you upstairs and find out what your whole body tastes like. But we can't give in now. We are too close to making it right." She agrees with me.

"I know, I just couldn't stop myself, and I don't regret it. Kissing is not against the law, now is it?"

"No, but where the kissing leads us is what's against the law. Believe me, that kiss was leading us right down on the hay. I told you, when I take you to make you completely mine, it will be in a bed." She smiles that, fuck-me smile and I swear my dick is going to cum right here in my jeans.

"You think I could borrow that book before that day comes?"

"What am I going to do with you, beautiful?"

I hear the other horses stir and that means someone they don't know is in the barn. I whisper in Jenna's ear to hide in the corner and be very quiet. I push open the gate and walk out a ways.

I say, "Hello? Who's there?" I wait a few seconds, before I see Amanda walk out of the dark.

"Hey sexy, you missed me?" I shake my head.

"What are you doing here?"

My phone vibrates in my pocket, so I pull it out and I swear my heart stops as I read Jenna's text. "IT'S HER, IT'S HER. SHE IS THE ONE BRYSON." I reply back.

"Text my dad, tell him to call 911. Tell him to come to the barn. NOW." I make small talk with Amanda.

"Sure, I miss everyone but, my dad needs me here. I won't be going back this semester." Amanda, squints her eyes.

"That's not the story I got. I was told it was because of that little whore that was here trying to trap you. But no worries. I got rid of her, and I am sure she will never come back around here."

That bitch, I have never wanted to hit a woman like I want to hit her. I sure hope Dad hurries out here. I may take her down and beat her just to show her how much I hate her.

"So you're the reason she ran and says she will never come back?" She keeps walking towards me but I don't want her to see Jenna so I walk towards her.

Looking behind Amanda, I tell her, "You do know I don't love you, and I never will, right?" She laughs and I want to punch her.

"Oh, you do love me and always have. But those little bitches keep throwing themselves at you. They are keeping you from coming to me. You know I can keep you happy, unlike that slut you married. Getting her hooked on meth was the easiest thing to do. Noah wanted her, and I wanted you. We came up with a plan. Together, we got what we wanted. The only problem was that Noah couldn't provide her with enough meth to keep her happy. But believe me, I will keep you happy, and I will never let you go."

My dad grabs her from behind and brings her to the ground. I catch the rope from the stall, and we tie her hands and feet. She is fighting and screaming and says she will get me for this. Mom runs in, "The police are on the way. Bryson where is Jenna?" I run to the stall and find Jenna is hiding in the hay trembling, and crying.

I pull her in my arms, "It's all over baby. We have her restrained until the police get here. Come on let's get you in the house."

When we walk out Amanda's jaw finally closes, and I think she is in shock. I take this time to get a little revenge. "This, Amanda, is the woman that holds my heart, mind, and soul. You, Noah, and all the meth in the world couldn't keep us apart. So, this joke is on you. I hope you find your true love behind bars, because that's the only place you are going. I will make sure you never get out." She glares at me.

"Look at her Bryson, she is pathetic and she's not even your type. Brunettes are your type, that's why I have my hair colored three times a month. You also like it rough and in odd places. Do you think she will give you that?" I laugh at her. I leave Jenna next to mom. I squat down so I can tell her what I have to say.

"My type? You think you know my type, Amanda? Well you don't know shit. My type is a woman who stands by me no matter what life throws our way. She will love me and our children. She will go through hell for her family. She has strength, courage, and unconditional love. I thought I would never find that in a woman, and yes, I have been with many women. But, I've finally found that special woman for me. Nothing and no one, will ever come between us because we complete each other. Jenna and my baby she is carrying are my world. The last thing you or anyone else wants to do is fuck with her. Because so help me God, you may as well give your soul to the good Lord above, because your ass will be mine. So, if you know what's good for you, you will never come around her again."

As two officers run into the barn. We explain that Amanda is the one who assaulted Jenna and threatened her life and that there were reports already filed. The police officer unties Amanda and places her in handcuffs. After reading her rights to her, the officer tell us we need to come down to the station and fill out some paper work. I put my arm around Jenna and she lays her head on me. "It's all over, baby girl, and she will never touch you again."

As we walk off, I hear my dad tell the officer that Jenna is a minor and the cop tells him with that Amanda is looking at added years.

Amanda then screams, "A MINOR?   But, she's pregnant! How could she be a minor? I swear I didn't know she was underage. I would not have touched her if I knew that. Bryson, please help me I can't go to jail." I just keep walking. Then it hits me, I need to thank her. So I turn and look her dead in the eyes.

"Amanda, thank you. If you would not have gotten Leah out of my life, I would not have been free to fall in love with Jenna, who I know now is my forever." I turn and walk away.

Chapter 19

Bryson

I am so at ease lately with the way my life is going. I have two wonderful parents who support me in whatever I choose in life. Their guidance has been a big part of my goals. Today it's safe to say my goals have all fallen into place. Dad and I are working side-by-side, and I must say, hands-on work beats the shit out of a classroom and books. My father knows this surveying shit like he knows the back of his hand. My mother is guiding my girl every step of the way on how to care for our little princess. We still haven't finished the baby's room. Jenna has no idea about our surprise.

When Jenna first came to stay with my parents, my mom told her about the nursery, and how she keeps it locked so she hasn't asked any questions. Mom has finally accepted that it's time to prepare for grandchildren. She no longer wants a baby for herself. She is looking forward to being able to spoil her grandchildren and sending them home. Mom works the on the nursery while Jenna and I are out. I work on it when they go shopping. When we get back from the doctor today, Mom should have it ready for the reveal. I can't wait to see Jenna's face when she sees it.

The only thing we can't do that Mom wanted is put her name on the wall. That's only because Jenna hasn't let us know what she wants to name the baby. I have suggested naming her after her mother, and she says she is considering it. I know I will be happy with whatever it is as long as the last name is Alexander. We had a long talk about her naming me as the father. I finally convinced her that I love this baby already, and nothing would change that.

I text Mom when we are getting into Beaumont so she knows we are almost home. She replies back that everything is ready to go. I can't wait, Jenna is going to be so shocked.

"Bryson Erin, what is that smile on your face for?" Damn, I really need to watch my smiles around her, or I am going to spoil her birthday surprise, too.

"My Mom just texted me, and it made me feel like a teenager again." Hopefully that works. She smiles and shakes her head. She knows I'm a damn liar, and I can't lie to her, but I just leave it alone. I can tell her after the reveal.

I get her out of the truck, even though I had the steps installed. Now, I tell her I am fearful of her slipping, but I am just being selfish and want to hold her. She slides to me and I help her down. We walk in and Mom meets us at the door to find out what the doctor told us. Jenna tells her everything, except the questions I asked and I smile going to the kitchen to get a drink. Dad is in the kitchen, and tells me everything is ready for the surprise when we are.

"Jenna, Mom, Dad, and I have something we need you to see." Jenna gives me a confused look and says okay. I take her hand and lead her up the stairs, with Mom and Dad following. When we reach the room, I put my hand on the door and Jenna stops me.

"Bryson, don't you know this room is off limits to everyone. Please, respect your mom's wishes and don't go in there." That's my girl, so smart and considerate of others.

"Well, Mom is right behind us, and has giving me permission, okay?" She turns to Mom, and Mom nods with tears in her eyes.

I open the door and watch her face. Shocked is an understatement. She turns to me, then to Mom, and the tears are flowing like rain.

"Kristi, are you sure? I can put her in the room with me. I know what this room means to you."

My mom cries and tells her, "Jenna this is my granddaughter, and besides you, she will be the daughter I never had. Who better to have my special room than our little princess?" She hugs us all and thanks us.

We all step into the room and look around. Jenna points to something on the wall. When I realize what she is pointing at, I think I have just been hit with a sledge hammer. On the wall is the baby's name. Mom has pink and white letters, and I can't believe what I am seeing.

I look at Jenna and she nods, "That's her name,Erin Elizabeth Kingsley-Alexander."

Now, it's my turn to cry and my mom says, "Surprise!"

We all laugh but, I have to ask Jenna. "Are you sure this is what you want, baby?" She shakes her head yes, still crying.

"Bryson, I have never in my life been more sure about something like I am about her name. She will carry four names of people I will always be thankful for, Erin after her father, Elizabeth after her three grandmothers, and Kingsley-Alexander after her grandfathers. Thank you all for everything, and I am glad to call you my family. I really hope you don't mind that I want her to carry both our last names so that the Kingsley name can be carried on a bit longer." I grab her face and kiss her hard. I love this woman with everything that I have.

When we come up for air I tell her, "Baby, you have just made me the happiest man alive. I am honored to have the Kingsley name attached to mine. Thank you so much, and I love you, Jenna. Today, tomorrow and forever."

Today is my Jenna's birthday, so I jump up and go down to get Mom. I need her to help me prepare a special breakfast in bed for Jenna. I burn my hand twice while frying the bacon. Shit, how do women do this without burning themselves? I get everything loaded on the tray with a rose from Mom's bushes. I am about to head up when Mom stops me. She puts a big glass of coffee milk on the tray. I can't believe I had forgotten the coffee milk.

I go up the stairs as slow as I can so I don't spill anything. I open the door, and Jenna is sitting in her bed staring at her phone.

"Happy Birthday, Baby." She looks up at me with a small smile and I know something must be wrong. "What's wrong?" It's obvious her heart is heavy for some reason.

"I texted Angel to see if she would have lunch with us today for my birthday, and she told me she didn't remember my birthday was today and she has already made other plans with Amy." Shit, that's my fault. Angel is just throwing her off because we have a big surprise party planned for her here tonight. Angel and Amy along with Bryan, Caden, Ethan, and Ramie will be here later today. I invited Ethan and Ramie, because I really want her to get to know my friends better, and I want to get to know Angel.

"I'm sorry, baby, but if it makes you feel better I am happy I will have you all to myself now that you are eighteen." I raise my eyebrows a couple of times and then give her a wink. Her face blushes but the smile grows bigger.

"I kinda waited for you to come in and attack me after midnight, but you never came." Damn, why didn't I think of that? I could have had my baby hours ago.

"I am going to take you, and make you mine when you least expect it, my love. Now, eat your breakfast so we can get our day started."

Jenna digs in and eats every bite. I let her know I cooked it all with Mom's supervision. "Well, I am impressed, Cowboy." She smiles that evil smile.

"Get up and get dressed while I will run down and clean up my mess. Once you're ready, we can go down and see Butta and Bella before we go out for the day." I have to remember not to push her too much so her feet don't swell. Jenna gets tired a lot faster since she is so far along. She only has a little over a month before our little Erin comes into our world. Man, I can't wait.

After checking on the horses we let Mom know we are going on a birthday date. Once in the truck, I ask her what she wants to do.

"Can we go visit my father's lawyer to see what I have to do to be able to drive my car again?" This will take up a good amount of time so Mom and the others can get things ready.

"Sure, baby. Can you give him a call and see if he will be able to see you today?" She makes the call and it's said that he can see her today at 11:00, so that will give us a couple of hours to do something else.

"So what do you want to do until then? It's your day so you can choose anything."

She taps her chin like she is thinking hard. "Can we go to my house in Houston?" Doesn't she know I would take her to the moon if she wanted to go?

"Of course, baby. I don't have a problem with that." I give her a wink, and we're off to Houston.

As we pass through her neighborhood, she wants me pass by Angel's house to see if she's home. When she doesn't see her car there she seems sad. "I can't believe I won't get to see her today. This is the first time in 13 years that we are not together for my birthday." Damn, I want to tell her just so she is not sad anymore, but I know the surprise later will be worth a little sadness today.

We go into the house and I ask Jenna to show me around. This seems to pick up her spirits some. I got to see the pool and Jacuzzi first. She says it has been her favorite place since she was a kid. I notice there is a privacy fence around the entire back yard. Hmm, this is a great place for our baby to grow up. The pool has its own fence with locking gates so she would not be able to get to the pool. She would have to have an adult, but she could play in the yard.

Jenna hasn't decided where she wants to live yet. I am willing to live wherever she chooses. We can move here, or we can build on the ranch. I really don't care where we live as long as we are together. Jenna and I walk around inside and she explains different things, and memories she has. When we make it to her bedroom, I pick her up and set her on the bed. I am not sure what has come over me, but I just feel the need to hold her.

"It's about time you touched me. I was beginning to think that you changed your mind. I have been eighteen for about 8 hours now."

I look her in her eyes and tell her, "I told you it would be when you least expected it, and it would be in a bed." She giggles. Finally the wait is over and I am ready to make my girl all mine.

I kiss her slowly and she runs her fingers in my hair. I slip my hand up her dress and grab at her full breast. Damn, they are so firm and the perfect size. Breaking the kiss, I back up to take her dress off. Jenna grabs my hand to stop me.

"Bryson, I don't think you want to see what's under this dress." Oh I definitely want to see it.

"What do you mean? Of course, I want to see. I have been waiting patiently for this day." Her face is sad and I don't understand.

"I look like a whale. I have gained over 30 pounds, and my body is stretched. It's not very nice to look at." I grab her face and make her look at me.

"Baby you're beautiful to me. Remember, I didn't know the 'before pregnant' Jenna. I fell in love with you and your belly. I want all of you. Now."

She stands up and I think I've lost her, but she begins to pull her dress up. I help her pull it over her head. I go to my knees and I kiss her belly. "Baby, how could you think I wouldn't love this? Our baby girl is in here, and to me, that is the most beautiful thing in the world." I whisper to her belly, "Daddy loves you Erin." She removes her bra and reveals the most beautiful breasts I have ever seen, and I have seen many. Now, she is standing before me in only her white panties.

I lay Jenna back on the bed as I kiss her. I massage her breasts and rub my hand down her belly. She gives a little moan, and I know I can do better than that. I head south and rub my finger over her panties. She opens her legs and moans louder. Now, that's what I wanted to hear. I break the kiss and hurry to remove my clothes. I need to feel her skin on mine. I take everything off, but my boxers, and I slowly pull off her panties. Holy shit, she is so wet and ready. My dick is twitching so bad to feel her, but no way is it getting in before I taste her.

I am on my knees between her legs and I open them wider. I run my tongue between her lips and she squirms. I do it again and lap up her sweet wetness. I plunge my tongue inside her. She grabs for my head but her belly doesn't allow her to reach me.

"Relax baby, and hold the sheets because I plan on taking you for a ride like you never had before." Continuing my assault inside her, I feel her squirm, and raise her hips. I know it won't be long now. I run my tongue over her clit and she screams.

"Yes, baby, there!" I suck her clit and give it a little bite and she screams a bit more. I decide it's time to take her higher, so I bring my finger to her entrance and enter her pussy in one motion. She wraps her legs around my neck and pulls my head closer. I add another finger and start working them. "Oh my God, Bryson, pleaaasee don't stop!" I suck harder on her clit before I remove my face and use my thumb to give a little pressure on her clit, and her cum spills out in a gush. I remove my fingers and lick her release.

Her body goes limp and I know she enjoyed her first orgasm with me. I remove my boxers, and lay beside her.

"Baby, you taste sweeter than I could have ever imagined, and I plan on tasting you every chance I get." She opens her eyes and rubs her hand thru my hair.

"Bry, I never knew my body was capable of doing what you made it do." I smile and give myself a "Dat-a-boy".

"That's only the beginning, baby."

I press my hard dick into her thigh and Jenna looks down. Her eyes go wide and I know what she's thinking. "It's going to fit, baby, I promise. Your body will adjust and I will take it slow. I promise, within two minutes you will be asking for more." Her face softens. Now, comes the tricky part being that I have never been with a pregnant woman. I need to be careful on so many levels.

I stand up, pulling her to the edge of the bed and she tightens up. "Relax. baby, I promise I won't hurt you."

I massage her tits as my cock lies on her pussy. I remove my hand and place my dick at her entrance and rub her clit. She is so wet, so I slowly push the head into her entrance. Damn, she is so tight. I push my dick in inch by inch until I am buried deep inside her. I lean over on my hands so I can see her face. "You okay, baby?" She gives me a nod and a smile and I start pulling out and push back in. Soon we start our rhythm and she is meeting me in the middle. Just like I promised earlier, Jenna begins to go faster, so I go a little faster and harder. I grab her knees so that I can give her what she's going to need to cum.

"Harder, baby, please! Harder!" That lets me know I need to up my rhythm, and we are both getting close. I know I can't, and don't, want to hold out any longer, so I take my thumb and put just the right amount of pressure on her clit. Jenna, cums while screaming my name, and clawing my arms. I give it two more pumps, and I release deep inside my girl. This is my woman, my forever.

Smiling at each other, I see the tears rolling down and I freak out. Pulling out of her I ask, "Oh, baby, did I hurt you? I'm so sorry, baby." She shakes her head no.

"I love you so much, Bryson, it hurts. I never thought I would find love like this. I thought for sure it was always going to be me and my baby. I never dreamed the most wonderful man in the world would walk in. Now, here you are making all of my dreams come true." She thinks I am fulfilling her dreams? I think it's the other way around. I am the luckiest man alive.

"Baby, I am the lucky one, but I promise I will try my hardest to do what I have to so you can live your dreams."

I head to Jenna's bathroom to grab a towel to clean her up when I hear her turn on the shower. "Baby girl, I don't think we have time to get a shower. If you get in that shower, I am coming with you, and I can't promise I will be able to let you go in time for us to make your appointment." She gives me her fuck me eyes, again, and I'm a goner.

"Then we will just have to make another one won't we?" That's all she had to say before I pick her up and walk us under the spray of hot water.

After a little playing in the shower, we wash up quickly and dress, trying to hurry so we can make it to the appointment. Jenna makes a quick call to Michelle, the receptionist at Rick's office, and tells her we are on our way but are stuck in traffic, so we will be a little late. I have to laugh because, if my little tiger wouldn't have put her lips on my dick while washing my legs, we would have made it on time. I will have to ask her one day where she learned to give a blow job like that. I didn't cum in her mouth, but damn, she sure worked it over like a pro.

We make to Rick's office, only a few minutes late. I felt sorry for Jenna when she found out she had to go into foster care for no reason. On the other hand, I am glad she did because I would never have met her. I know she had a hard time in the first month or so, but it lead her to me. Jenna gets all of the answers she needs, and he promises to contact her when all the paperwork is ready.

The steakhouse we go to is awesome and they cook my steak just like I like it. Not many places have done that. We have a good talk and I find out more things about her. I don't think I will ever get enough of this woman, she just amazes me. We finish up and now I am taking her to the mall so I can give mom and the others time to set up.

We get into the mall and I see a jewelry store. I lead us in and her eyes grow wide. "No, baby, not a ring but I would love to have something around your neck that will be a symbol of our love until that day comes." The smile fades and I want to tell her but I don't. I have to keep telling myself, that it will be worth it. We choose together an infinity sign with little diamond on half of each side. I put it on her neck and I know it's perfect. Her smile is back, and I know she is good for now.

We walk around going into a few places and Jenna buys a few things for Caden and the girls. I get her to buy some nice nightgowns and a robe for when she delivers the baby. I have seen her night clothes, and it's not something a mother wears in the hospital after having a baby.

I get a text from Mom asking me if I had made up my mind yet. I text Mom back "yes", and then I type in "I AM GOING TO DO IT!" Only Mom and I know what that means.

She texts me back saying we can start back home now, but we need to let her know when we are about a mile away.

"Baby, I think we need to get you home before your feet start to swell. I want you well rested tonight when I take you out for your special birthday dinner." That smile tells me she is more than ready. As we pass Dip 'N Dots she looks at me with those puppy dog eyes.

"Jenna my love, if you want some we can get you some, and you know that. Please, don't give me those sad eyes." She smiles, and we go to the counter. I would buy this woman the stars if she wanted them. We get her order and head back to the truck. She climbs in on my side, and I love the fact that she wants to sit close to me. I help her into the truck, and get her seatbelt on.

"Bryson, I talked to Kathie yesterday, and I finally told her about the home Caden is in. I told her the truth of what goes on in that hellhole." I know that was hard for her because she worries so much about Caden being hurt there.

"What did she have to say, baby?" Jenna starts picking at her fingers. That lets me know it was hard.

"She told me that Caden will be in the foster system until he is eighteen. His mother was given a life sentence without parole. Kathie says the girls have a good chance of being adopted, but very slim chances on Caden." Damn, he is such a good kid.

"Are they going to move him now that you told her about the shit hole?" She doesn't answer right away.

"Kathie said she will investigate it. I sure hope I didn't start more trouble for Caden. He doesn't deserve that." I put my arm around her and pull her head to my chest.

"I am sure he will be fine, baby, Bryan will take care of him." We both go silent the rest of the way.

I texted Mom about a mile back, and everything is ready. We pull up at the house, and there are no cars around. I help her out of the truck, and get the bags from the mall. I go around to the front and open the glove box to get out my next surprise, and sneak it into my pocket. When we walk in the house all is quiet and we seem to be alone. I drop the bags on the couch and hug my baby.

I take both her hands in mine, and she looks up at me. "Jenna, baby, you have brought me back from the dead. You made me want to live again. I never believed I could, or would, ever love again. When I laid eyes on you at the top of that staircase, I thought I was dreaming. You walked into my life, stole my heart, and repaired a man who was so broken."

I get down on my knee, and look up to her. "Jenna, I love you and I love our baby girl you're carrying. What I want to know now, is, will you make me the happiest and luckiest man on Earth and be my wife, my forever?" I pull open the box. She puts one hand over her mouth and the other on her belly, and cries.

"Yes, yes I will marry you, Bryson!" I stand up and put the ring on her finger and everyone yells "SURPRISE." Jenna jumps into my arms, and I steady her. She cries more as she looks around the room.

All our friends are here, and they come to say congratulations. After all the hugs and tears, and everyone checking out her ring, Caden walks over and wants her to open his gift to her. Caden had contacted me, and was upset because he had no money to get her anything. Mom and I came up with a perfect gift we knew she would love. The day in the park we had with Caden and his sisters, Mom got a great shot on her camera, of Jenna with the three kids on the swing. They all had great smiles, and it's one of those priceless moments. Mom and Caden took the picture and had it blown up and framed while we were out.

"Oh my, Caden, this is beautiful and I will hang it so I can see it every day. Thank you so much. This means the world to me." I have no doubt she will have this in the living room.

Mom announces it's time to sing "Happy Birthday", so we all go to the dining room where all of the decorations, cake and presents are. We sing 'Happy Birthday' and make Jenna blow out the candles.

"I have everything I could ever want here in one room. I have nothing to wish for, but I want to thank you all so much for everything." That's my baby, always thinking nothing could make her happier.

I whisper in her ear. "So, when will you marry me?" She turns in my arms so she is facing me and whispers back to me.

"Anytime you want, cowboy."

I whisper, "Tomorrow."

She pulls away and shouts, "Tomorrow?"

Everyone gets quiet and looks at us. Mom knows exactly what this is about. I married Leah the day after I proposed. We went to the courthouse in Baton Rouge and got married before I called mom to let her know.

"Bryson Erin, if you think you are going to have another twenty-five dollar wedding at the courthouse, you are dead wrong. You are my only child. I only have one shot at a beautiful church wedding. And you, my son, will not take that away again." I know she is serious so I give her a little smile and throw her for a loop.

"Well, lovely mother of mine, you have until December 31st for this wedding of your dreams to take place. If we are not married by then, we will be married on New Year's Day. If I have to fly us to Vegas to do it, I will." Her eyes squint and I know she is mad.

"I will take that challenge, butt head son of mine. I will pull off the perfect wedding." Everyone now laughs and joins in on the conversation.

"Bryson can I see Bella like you promised? Jenna says she is getting big now." I look down into Caden's blue eyes and there is no way I can say no.

"Sure thing, buddy, let's go." Once Caden lays eyes on all of the horses, this kid doesn't know what to say or where to go. I take him to meet Bella and Butta, and he asked if I could one day teach him to ride. That gets me a big smile and I promise him once things calm down around here, and Jenna has the baby, we will get him here to ride. He is content with that. Now, I see why he holds a piece of my Jenna's heart.

"Let's go back and get us a piece of cake, Buddy. I am sure you are ready for that." Caden smiles and runs for the house.

Now that everyone has eaten cake and the mounds of presents were opened, I think they are all partied out. Ethan and Ramie say they need to get going, so Jenna and I walk them out. While telling them goodbye, Bryan and Caden come from the house to say goodbye too. Bryan says they will keep in touch. After Jenna gives Caden hugs, she waves as they drive away. Jenna and I walk back in and Mom and Dad let us know they are headed out for a late night movie. I know they are only giving us some time alone. Once they are gone I pick up my love and take her to her room.

"What do you say to a movie in my room?" She gives me those damn eyes. "Baby, if you don't stop look at me with them puppy dog eyes we are never going to watch a movie." She gives me a wink and it's on.

"Forget the pjs. Come with me." I take her to my room, handing her one of my t shirts, and, for the second time today, I help lift her dress over her head.

"I know you're tired, so I will just help you get dressed, but you need to know I want to lay you in my bed and take us both into a state of bliss." She looks at me as she removes her bra.

"Who says I'm too tired? I will never be too tired to make love to my soon to be husband." That's all I needed to hear, and I have her in my arms and on the way to my bed. I take her panties off and throw them, God knows where, and I am between her legs as fast as I can. This woman has no idea what she does, to me.

"Uhm, Bryson it's not that what you're doing doesn't feel amazing. It really does but can you please just make love to me now?" What my baby wants, she gets. I take off my clothes and join her in the bed.

"I sure wish this stomach of mine wasn't so big, so I could feel your body next to mine." I think of what I can do to solve that problem.

"Baby, I can take you from behind where your back can be up against my chest if you want?"

"Okay, let's try it." I roll her on her side and open her legs rubbing my dick over her wet pussy until she says "Now, please." I push it in and I go all the way. I slowly make love to her with my chest against her back. When she can't take it anymore and says she needs more. I pull out and lay on my back.

"Climb up here and straddle me, baby. I will let you ride me so you can control it and take what you need." She straddles me and I pick her up and set her on my dick.

She slowly goes all the way down my dick and starts to grind. I think I am going to lose my shit. I begin to move picking her up and setting her down. Our rhythm gets faster and harder, and I am not going to last. I give her clit a pinch and she cums exploding on my dick but never stops "Cum with me, Bry. Please." Bam her words are music to my ears, and I give her every drop I have.

"God, I love you so much, Jenna. I think you are my new addiction." She gives me a wink.

"That's an addiction I will never complain about, I promise." I remove her from my dick and we walk to the shower. I don't think she can take anymore today, but I won't turn her down if she wants more.

Jenna

Today I go to see Dr. Lacy I can't believe it's been six weeks since I have been here. Time is moving so fast now that my life is normal. Well, I say normal when I should say not so eventful, now that Amanda is behind bars and can't hurt anyone.

Bryson has started helping his dad with the ranch and the business. Kristi and I have been some shopping to get things ready for the baby to come. I got a surprise call during the week from Caden. It seems that wonderful man of mine thinks of everything. He gave him a cell phone just so he could call or text me. I had planned to get him one when I was there but was taken away before I got around to it. He wanted to know when we could meet again. He misses me and just wants to spend time together. Bryson said he would take me to see him anytime I wanted so we made plans for next week when Bryan is off.

Bryson and I have really gotten to know each other. We take long walks in the pasture. I have given him my life story. Well as far back as I can remember. I shock him a few times but it was fun. He has told me everything about Leah. How they had made plans for the future. I asked him if he feels bad now that he knows what Amanda and Noah did to her.

"It's not right what they did. I believe in faith. I think everything happens for a reason. I always asked God why. Now I know why. I had to be ready for you. I don't regret any of it." He is so amazing and I can't think of another person I would want to spend the rest of my life with.

Dr. Lacy says everything is fine and my weight gain is perfect. The baby is at a good size and she asked if I had any questions. I tell her no, and let her know that everything is fine except the swelling in my feet at times. She said swelling is normal but to keep an eye on them changing colors. When she gets up to leave Bryson asks if he could speak to her alone. I swear if he thinks I am leaving this room so he can talk to my doctor he is so dead wrong. She tells him "Bryson, I can answer questions you have alone only if they do not pertain to Jenna." Ha now take that shit Mr. *I want to get her back*.

But I shit when he says, "Okay I will ask with her here. What about sex? Is that something she can do until the birth or will it harm her or the baby?" Oh. My. God. He did not just ask that. Dr. Lacy looks at us both with a little grin on her face.

"Sex is fine as long as you don't get too rough or over creative with it. The baby is protected so a normal sex life can continue up until birth." I know my face is fifty fricken shades of RED. He gives me and wink and says we can go now.

We thank Dr. Lacy and go to make my next appointment. Why would he ask her that? Then it hits me we are less than two weeks away from my birthday. Holy Shit, what have I signed up for here?

When we get home I am surprised with the most beautiful nursery any mother could ask for. Everything is pink and white from the walls down to the rugs on the floor. I know how much this room meant to Kristi so her giving it up for my baby means so much to me. Kristi and John are going to be the best grandparents in the world. Not to mention Bryson will be an outstanding dad. I loved the look on his face when he seen her name I have chosen for her. His tears said it all but he sealed it with a kiss I never knew was possible.

Waiting for my birthday is getting harder and harder. I take a few pictures and send them to Caden. I know he'll love it. He sends me a text back that just says "WOW!" Poor little boy I sure hope one day he will have a room he can be proud of. Now that the baby's name is out I text him and tell him. Of course he doesn't know what all the names mean to me. I explain it to him. Finally he calls me because he is tired of typing. We talk for a bit and I tell him I will see him in a few days. "Bye Jenna I love you." I don't think I will ever tire of that kid telling me he loves me.

"I love you too baby boy."

Today is my eighteenth birthday and it gets off to a bad start. I text Angel and ask if she would have lunch with us. She says she forgot it was my birthday and she has made plans with Amy. I think I have been replaced as BFF and I don't like that feeling. Bryson walks in with a tray full of food and beautiful rose. I try to smile but he knows something isn't right. I explain my sadness and as always he has a way of making things better. I am starving so I eat everything and drink my awesome coffee milk. I know he has not made because only Kristi and my mom makes it perfect. I can't even make it this good. But I don't tell him I know better. He tells me to get ready that we will check on the horses. Then we will spend the day doing whatever I want to do.

I am dressed and ready to go in no time. I just can't wait to spend the day with my man legally. I know that sounds funny but to us it means a lot. I really want to see what I have to do to get my car into my name. I don't like having to depend on everyone to taxi me around. After that I will let him bring me wherever he wants. I am a little disappointed that he hasn't touched me yet. I was hoping after midnight he would have snuck into my room for a little play time but that didn't happen. I know I could have gone to him but mom always told me *"don't chase boys Jenna let them chase you. A true gentleman will always come to his lady."* So I just stayed and waited and I'm still waiting but hoping he makes his move soon.

I call and make an appointment with Rick. He is dad's lawyer and military brother. His secretary says he can fit us in. The only problem is we have a couple of hours before we see him. Now I am not sure what to do. I decide that we can go to my house in Houston. Angel is not home so I am sure she is with Amy but I won't let that ruin my day. Once at my house I give Bryson a tour of the backyard and then the house. When we get inside my room he picks me up and puts me on my bed. I am so ready for him to take me. I hold back in hopes he makes the first move. If he doesn't my next stop will be a sex store so I can get something to help me find my release.

Well the wait is over when he removes my clothes. I feel like a whale but he makes me feel so sexy at the way he looks at me. He has magic hands that set my body on fire. Lord have mercy the things this man can do with his mouth is heavenly. My first time with sex was just that sex but this.., this is love and he makes me feel like I am his world. The things he tells me and the way he works my body brings tears to my eyes. I love this man so much it hurts. After we make love we go to the shower. A girl could get used to being bathed by her man.

Giving my first blow job was simply amazing. I never thought I would ever put something like that in my mouth. With Bryson it didn't feel dirty. When he tells me he will cum soon I want to taste him but at the last minute I get scared and pull it out. He doesn't seem upset. His release is something I am glad I was able to watch. I think I am addicted to him and this only makes me happier than I was before.

After we dry off and dress we need to hurry to Rick's office so we are not late. I throw my hair up in a clip and we are off. I call the office and let Michelle know we are stuck in traffic and will be a little late. She says its fine and he will be waiting for us.

Michelle greets us and says he will be with us shortly. We take a seat and I go through all the papers I found in dad's desk. I have the deed for the house and all the titles on the vehicles we owned. I found three accounts that belonged to mom and dad. I know he also has a stock account I am hoping Rick will be able to find. "Jenna, so nice to see you come on in." Rick greets me with a hug and I introduce him to Bryson. We have a seat in his off and he begins.

"Jenna I had no idea you were expecting. I tried to reach you a few times since your parents passing but was unsuccessful. Your father's Will leave's everything to you and your mother. It also states that if your mother is deceased it is all to go to you. I can start the paperwork on having everything transferred in your name. Once it's all done you can come back and finalize it all." I am okay with that but I want to know what I am allowed to do with it until then.

"So until it's all finial what limits do I have?" His gets this puzzled look on his face.

"What limits are you talking about, Jenna?"I can't get over the look on his face.

"Well I know I am not able to drive my car but what about the house?" He gives me a more confusing look.

"What do you mean you can't drive your car?" I explain that I was told I couldn't have my car because it was under my father's name and I had to wait till I was eighteen to put into my name.

He takes a deep breath "Jenna I am not sure who gave you that information but that's not true. Had I known you were told this I would have cleared it up before now. I figured you were going through a hard time and would come when you were ready. However I did go by your house a few times but you were never home." Wait is this man telling me I could have had my car, and stayed in my home all this time?

"Rick what are you saying? I was taken from my home five days after my parents were killed. I was told I had to go into foster care until I was eighteen." He shakes his head and proceeds to tell me.

"You were in a foster home all this time for no reason. If I had known this I could have stopped it. There was no reason for you to be in a home. Like I said had I known I would have gone to the judge to keep you in your home. See Jenna, your father and I had a conversation about this year's ago. Knowing the situation of you all not having much family I made sure your dad and mom gave power of attorney to someone in case of an accident such as this one. I had full power, and I could have had you emancipated." Bryson squeezes my hand and I look at him. I am shocked, angry, confused. After thinking a bit on the information I hear Bryson say.

"No use in living the past baby things happen for a reason." He's right and if they wouldn't have taken me I would had never met him or Caden.

"Yes it's best just to move on. So, I can drive my car and stay in my home before you get this all changed over?" Rick smiles.

"Yes ma'am and I will let you know when I need you back in. Give me a number where I can contact you. In the meantime I have a check here from your parent's life insurance. They paid all the funeral services and sent the remaining balance in your name and mine. I can either get you to sign it and I can write you a check from my account. Or I can have Michelle deposit it directly into your account. It's all up to you. Do you need any money now? I have cash here on hand"

I am trying to process everything he just said. "No Rick I am fine daddy always made sure I had money in my account. Thank God that wasn't frozen. You can just have Michelle deposit in my account." I give him my account number along with my phone number.

"Jenna the check is a very large amount. Your father always worried about you and your mom's future. He made sure it would be enough to get you all though your lifetime. To top it off it was an accidental death so it was doubled." That's how my father's mind worked. He always worried about his girls. I look at the man on my side, and I know he too will take care of his girls. How did I get so lucky? I give Rick a hug and we say good bye.

Bryson and I are both pretty quiet until we get in the truck. Bryson pulls me next to him and kisses my head. "I know you went through hell in the first home and I hate that.

I keep thinking if you were not put in my mother's home I never would have met you. I would still be lost and broken and you would be alone."

I kiss him and tell him, "I don't regret any of it, Bryson. Not even the first home, if I wouldn't have been placed there I would not have met Caden." We smile at each other and he gently touches my face.

"Baby, I have told you how beautiful you are?"

"Yes, you always say that, even though I think you're crazy, it makes my day."

"Get used to it beautiful, because I plan on making your day every day." I reach over and give him a kiss, and he turns in his seat and kisses back. I wonder if he is as ready for another round as I am?

When we come up for air he says, "Baby, if we don't stop now I will be looking for a country road to take you on. Besides I think we need to get you something to eat." I laugh because I think it's more like he needs to eat.

I give him directions to Morton's because I know how he loves steak. I have already brought him to Vic & Anthony's so this is the next best steaks in Houston. He is worried that we are not dress up. I tell him he is fine and I don't care what people think. We eat and talk about things in our future. He asked if I know where I want to live. If I want to stay in Houston or we can build a house on the ranch by his parents. I really don't care either way as long as I'm living with him. But I don't want to get rid of my parent's home. We can keep it or rent it out but I don't want to sell it.

"Do you ever go to Galveston, you know to the beach?" A cocky smile comes across his face.

"I love Galveston beach and Ethan and I had planned to spend a couple of weeks there. We were going to rent a beach house so we could have parties every night." I raise my eyebrows and bite my bottom lip.

"Well what happen to them plans?" I wait for sarcastic comeback.

"Oh some beautiful bare footed pregnant angel appeared at the top of my staircase and totally captured my heart and mind." I laugh but then I decide to see if I can blow him away again.

"Well after the baby's born we could go and spend as long as you want rent free." He squints his eyes then raises an eyebrow.

"You want to explain that one baby?" Here comes the fun part.

"Well you see after all the paperwork is done you are looking at the owner of a five bedroom beach house." His eyes grow large and he shakes his head.

"Will the surprises ever stop with you? Every time I turn around you throw me something different." All I can do is shrug my shoulders. "Come on let's go shopping and see if we can find you a birthday present you don't have already."

Once inside the mall Bryson spots a jewelry store. He pulls me into the store and of course I think he's going to buy me a ring. Well that wasn't the case. I was a little upset but, the necklace he bought me is beautiful. I have always loved the infinity symbol, and so does Bryson.

We walked in and out of so many stores I thought my feet were going to fall off. I knew he wanted us to spend the day together so I kept my mouth shut and kept shopping. Finally he says he wants to go home and get some rest before we go out to eat. Thank God I am so over all this shopping.

We get home and all the lights are out, and Kristi's car is gone. We get in the house and he drops all the bags on the sofa. Bryson grabs both my hands and starts telling me how much I have changed his life and how much he loves me. I can't say a word. When he goes down I think he is going to talk to the baby but when he asks me to be his wife. I think my whole body goes numb. I answer as fast as I can. And like that wasn't enough all our friends and his parents come out of hiding and yell "SURPRISE" I throw myself into Bryson's arms. I don't think my legs are going to hold me up anymore. I cry because I am happy. I cry because his words were beautiful. I cry because my parents are not here to see me on the happiest day of my life. I cry because my best friend did not forget my birthday. Angel is here to celebrate the happiest day of my life.

My precious little Caden comes up and gives me a hug and wants me to open his present. I open it up and tears just come as they wish. As I look at the snap shot Kristi had blown up of Caden, Gaby, Jazzy and me at the park. It's beautiful and I tell him I will hang it where I will see it every day and I will.

Everything was beautiful the cake the decorations and oh my goodness the presents. I thought I would never get to the end. After we ate and everyone got their cake we walked out to the barn so Caden can meet Bella. He was floating on cloud nine with all the horses. My Bry, promises to teach him to ride one day and his face lights up. I love that smile. We make our way back to the house and everyone is pretty tired and ready to go. We walk them all out to their cars. Which were parked behind the barn earlier and they leave. Kristi and John have a date so it only leaves Bryson and I. Hmm I wonder if that's the ending to my surprise day.

We go up to my room I grab my comfortable PJ's so I can relax and watch a movie. I don't think he likes my choice. He hauls me into his room and shows me one of his big t-shirts which will fit me like a night gown. He removes all my clothes and I help him remove his and this man's body blows my mind. He has perfect abs. His arms are so big and firm. His shoulders are spread out, but must of all his eyes. His eyes you have to look into to see the true color. You think they are brown but you look again and they are green.

This gorgeous man takes me to bed where he makes love to me nice and slow. I never thought I would like being on top but I do. I hope he lets me do that often. When we are done we hit the shower and you already know what happens there. We fulfill our addiction.

Chapter 20

Jenna

Today is hopefully our last visit with Dr. Lacy. I only have two weeks left so we have been seeing her every two weeks. She lets me know I am dilated two centimeters. She thinks I should stay close until the birth. Once we leave the office Bryson and I talk about what we should do from here. "We can pack some clothes and stay at my house here in Houston where we can be close to the hospital. Or we can hope the baby stays in long enough for you to get us here from Beaumont." He looks terrified and it's funny.

"I think staying in Houston is better all the way around. If mom wants she can stay with us too. I agree I have no problems with her staying.

Bryson and I hired a painter to come in and paint the house in colors we liked and we changed all the furniture so we could make the house ours. I know my mom and dad wouldn't mind. I know they would want me to be happy here. Bryson and I bought a beautiful new bedroom set and we are taking the master bedroom. We turned dad's office into a nursery for Erin. Once she is old enough she can go into one of the other rooms. We made the decision to stay at the ranch for at least two weeks after the baby is born. Then we will come back to Houston.

We are still trying to decide if we want to build a house on the ranch or not. Bryson says we can wait until after we are married and things settle down before we make up our minds. The baby is due on September 30th but I don't see it going that long. The wedding is planned for December twenty-second and Bryson is content with that. Kristi swears everything will be perfect for our special day. I really don't care about a big wedding as long as he promises to love me and be beside me for the rest of our lives then I am good.

"Well let's head back to Beaumont and give mom the news. She can make up her mind on what she wants to do. We can pick up the bags we have packed for the hospital and pack more for us to stay until then. Everything is set up at both houses so we shouldn't have any problems." My man always thinks of everything I swear I don't understand how I lived without him, but I damn sure know I never want to live without him again.

"Bryson baby wake up, baby I need you to wake up. I think we need to go the baby is coming." He jumps from the bed.

"Are you sure? How do you know? Are you hurting? Did your water break?"I give him my puppy eyes that always calm him.

"Slow down baby you're making me dizzy. I have been hurting for a couple of hours now. I have been pacing the hallway. I felt a lot of pressure and water came gushing I think my water broke." The horror in his eyes says he is scared to death.

"My God Jenna why didn't you wake me or mom? Why would you do this all alone baby? Let me wake up mom and we will get you changed and ready to go."

My poor baby this is why I didn't wake him he would have rushed me in to wait for hours. Kristi comes in and helps me in a clean dress and wipes down my legs. Bryson gets the bags into the truck and comes back for me. He tries to carry me but I tell him it's better for me to walk. He holds on to me like I am going to drop at any minute. This delivery is going to be so much fun with him. Poor Dr. Lacy I sure hope she is ready for this cowboy.

After they load me in the truck Bryson and I head for the Hospital with Kristi behind us in her SUV. We make it to the hospital and Bryson starts barking orders. My poor man he's a wreck. He called Dr. Lacy three times on the trip up here to make sure she was on her way. When he sees her he relaxes a bit and lets her take over. They get me admitted and into a room and start with all the monitors. I am at eight centimeters and she wants to know if I want an epidural. If I have come this far I think can make it.

"Baby please don't put yourself through too much pain I don't think I can handle you hurting." I wave him down for a kiss and whisper.

"I will be fine just hold, my hand and don't leave me." He gives me the weakest smile possible.

"Oh my love nothing and nobody could get me one step away from you. I will be here the whole time I promise." He kisses me and holds my hand.

Angel comes running in. "Is she here did I miss it?" We all turn and laugh and shake our heads. "Oh shit I thought for sure I was going to be late. How did I know you would wait until two o'clock in the damn morning to go into labor?" I just shrug my shoulders and breathe through another contraction.

"That was the hardest one yet" Kristi says as she watches the machine.

About 45 minutes later I can't go anymore and Dr. Lacy walks in. "My nurse tells me it's time to meet your baby girl are you ready, Jenna?" Hell yeah I am ready what the hell does she think?

"Pass ready doc let's get her out." Bryson is at the end of his calmness. "Can we push now for God's sakes she has been in pain too long. You need to do something."

I squeeze his hand and tell him, "I am fine and Bry, it's almost over baby." He tries hard to smile, but he can't.

"Okay Jenna on the next contraction you are going to push and count to ten then breathe. Ready?" I nod my head and push and I hold on to Bryson and Angels hands.

They count to ten for me and I lay back. "Very good, now we are going to do that again on the next one." We do this four or five more times when I hear Bryson.

"I see her baby I see her! Come on you can do it baby." I give one more big push and she's out. Bryson cuts the cord and she begins crying. I swear that is the sweetest sound. Bryson grabs my face and kisses me. "You did it my baby love you did it. She's here and she's perfect just like you."

I start to cry and I want to see her. Dr. Lacy hands her to Bryson and he brings her to my chest. "Hi Erin my little princess this is your mommy and she is the best." He hands her to me and we all cry together.

"She's beautiful Bryson, our baby girl is beautiful." He wipes the tears from his eyes.

"Just like her mom." The nurse takes her to clean her up and get her weight. I hear a tap on the door and Bryson goes to see who it is. He waves them in. It's Caden and he runs to me.

"Are you ok Jenna? Is baby Erin ok too? Can I see her? Can I do something for you? Are you hurting?" Bryson steps up.

"She's fine buddy everything is good and they are cleaning up the baby. When they are done we will see about letting everyone hold her okay?" His smile is from ear to ear.

"Sure Bryson I will go sit with Angel and wait for my turn." My sweet boy how did I get so lucky? I know everything happens for a reason.

Before long they bring her back all clean and hungry. Kristi holds her and passes her to Angel. Once Angel is done they let Caden have her. Finally my baby is in the arms of her daddy. I can breathe easy knowing he will never let anything happen to our little princess. "Jenna baby I love you and I can never thank you enough for making me the happiest man on Earth."

Bryson, Erin and I have moved to Houston. I am finishing my senior year at home and will walk with my graduating class. Bryson hasn't yet decided if he wants to finish off at LSU or here at one of the local colleges. I have told him I will support whatever decision. I even told him we would move with him to Baton Rouge until his graduation.

Erin is spoiled after her daddy and is definitely a daddy's girl. I know he will have her on a horse before she takes her first step. He and I have gone on a couple rides since I had Erin but I still haven't gone on a horse alone. I am sure with time I will get more comfortable. Maybe by that time Bella will be ready for me to ride her. Bryson says she's mine because she is hard headed and only listens to me.

I am cooking a seafood gumbo when I hear Erin wake up from her nap. Before I can wash my hands I hear. "Don't worry about her baby I'll get her." I should have known he would but I wasn't sure if he was in the house. He brings her in the kitchen so I can get some loving.

"Hey princess did mommy's baby sleep good?" She smiles and at me and my heart melts. Bryson and I have talked about having another baby soon. I know he wants a boy but you will never get him to admit to that. He says he will take whatever God gives us he just doesn't want Erin to be an only child.

Kristi and I have been planning a lot on the wedding. I am getting excited but she is on top of the world. She says she can't wait for Bryson to see me in my dress. He always says I was an angel sent here just for him. She says he will cry when he sees me. I don't doubt it at all. Bryson is a big strong man inside and out but when it comes to Erin and I he's a big softy. I must say for the record I wouldn't have him any other way. I never dreamed I would find a man that would love me and my baby. God has sent me way more than just a man. He sent me the best man. I couldn't ask for better and I know my mom and dad would love him as much as I do.

Today was one of the happiest days of my life. Since Bryson and I moved out of his parent's house. John and Kristi decided the house was too empty. Kristi spoke with Kathie and they are taking in Caden, Gaby and Jazzy. She said life without parent's had to be hard enough without having you siblings taken away too. So now they will be moving in and I can't wait to see them. Kristi and I have redecorated the rooms and bought them everything we could think of for them to play and be kids. I know Caden will love Kristi because she and I have the same heart. She is what he needs at this point in his life.

Bryson and I have talked about building the house on the ranch. Now that the kids are there I am more than sure I want it. I will never get rid of our house in Houston but people have more than one house. We will have three because I refuse to sell the beach house in Galveston too. I just can't wait for summer to come back around so we can all go and take the kids.

I hear the car pull up and I know they are here. "Bryson their here, bring the baby down so Kathie can see her." He must be upstairs because I don't see any mess down here.

"We coming mommy someone decided to give daddy a stinky diaper that leaked all over her pretty dress we had her in. I had to give her a bath and get her all prettied up again." I look up at them on the top of stairs and wish I had a camera. He talks to her like she's an adult as he walks her down the stairs.

Caden jumps from the van and runs in and wraps his arms around me. "I can't believe you did it Jenna. You promised me one day I would be with my sisters and now it's happening. I knew you were my guardian angel." Tears fill my eyes and I hug him tight.

"You were my saving grace kiddo and for that I will always be here for you." He kisses my cheek and heads to Bryson.

"Can I hold her Bryson? I promise I will sit down and I will hold her head so she doesn't hurt herself." Bryson looks at me and I nod.

"Sure buddy sit here and I will put her in your arms." He places him in Cadens arms and she starts to cry.

"It's ok Erin I am your big brother and I won't hurt you ever. I will protect you like I protected my sisters." She stops crying like she understands what he just said. My heart is so full seeing him smile.

The girls are a little shy but once we get the van unloaded and they see their things are here too they seem to relax more. After we speak to Kathie and Kristi signs all the paperwork Kathie says she has to go. We walk her out and thank her for everything she has done. "Jenna I just want to say thank you for everything. You speaking up have lead to the State revoking Louise and Clay's rights as foster parents. I am so sorry you went through what you did. I wish I could change that but I can't." I give her a hug and tell her.

"Everything happens for a reason and I don't regret it. If you would not have placed me there I would not have met these wonderful people and kids. Please don't be hard on yourself, but please let the state know they need to check these homes. These kids don't deserve homes like that." She agrees and says goodbye.

I wonder if there is something I can go to college for that will help to make sure what happened to Caden and I never happens to another child. I will definitely have to check into that. I want to be an inspector. I would make surprise visits. I would show up when they least expect me. I would also spend time with the children so they would feel safe to tell me. I would shut down a bad foster home in a minute and never feel bad about it. I only had over a month of one but I know I will never forget it as long as I live.

Once back in the house I see Bryson go up the stairs with Erin. I ask where he is going and she shushes me. That means she is back to sleep. Caden has gone out to the barn to find John. Kristi and I take the girls and their things and bring them up to see their new rooms. Cheryl said the girls never wanted to sleep apart so we have them a room set up together and the other room is set up as a play room. Gaby and Jazzy are really excited with both rooms. I really believe they will love it here all together.

I hear Caden call my name "Jenna where are you? Come down here please Mr. John and Bryson are going to put me on a horse. I want you to be there too." He is so excited and the words are going a mile a minute. I let him know I am on my way. Kristi grabs her camera and we go out to the barn. Bryson has the saddle on Butta but he also has a saddle on Ben.

"Why do you have them both of them saddled up?" He smiles his little evil smile.

"Because you're going on Butta and Caden is going on Ben." I do believe they had this planned.

"What makes you so sure I am going to get on that horse?" He walks towards me and I know there is no escape.

"Because you promised me, and I know you will never go back on your word." He's right I never want to put any doubt in his mind. I will go to the ends of the earth for this man day or night.

"Ok baby but if I fall and break anything you will be the one who will have to cook, clean, and take care of Erin." He laughs and assures me he is ok with that.

John helps Caden on while Bryson helps me. I am scared but I know he won't let anything happen to me. Butta is just as gentle as a lamb and makes me feel comfortable. They walk us around the ring a couple of times and then let us go. They tell us what to do at different times. Before long we are trotting around like we know what we doing. I can hear Caden's giggles and it's such an amazing sound. I know he is going to love it here. I think it's time to talk to Bryson about the ranch house.

I never believed I could be happy again after losing my parents. But these people have proved me wrong. My life is so complete now and I couldn't be any happier. I do miss my parents and wish they were here. I know in my heart they are watching over us.

We are now staying in Houston in Jenna's house so we can be closer to the hospital. I feel a tap on my arm and think I am dreaming. I hear her voice saying its time and her water broke. I jump from the bed and start looking for my clothes. She starts telling me she has been in labor for a couple of hours and I really start to freak. I throw on my clothes and run to wake up my mom. I take the bags to the truck while mom helps her to wash up and put a dress and clean panties on. Not sure why clean panties it's not like they will be on very long.

I run up to carry my baby down but she insists on walking so I just hold on so she has me to lean on. We get her in the truck and mom runs to her car. We take off and I call Dr. Lacy, Bryan and Caden, Ethan, Ramie and Angel. When we make it to the hospital these people don't move fast enough for me. Dr. Lacy meets us and gets her up to a room. After all the monitors are hooked up the damn pains get bad. I beg her to take something for pain but she refuses.

After what seems like forever it's time for her to push. After a few pushes I see her head. I coach her to keep pushing and her she comes slipping out like a blob of flesh. I wait for a cry like you hear on T.V. but it doesn't come. They hand me some scissors and tell me to cut here. I cut the cord and Dr. Lacy rubs under her foot and the crying begins. I let out a deep breath. The doctor hands her to me and I count ten fingers and ten toes and then I set her next to Jenna. She is so beautiful just like her mom. They come to get her to clean and weigh her so this gives me a few minutes to tell my woman how much I love her. After she is cleaned our friends and family pass her around and I can't wait for them to hand her back to me. Once in my arms I go to Jenna "Jenna baby I love you and I can never thank you enough for making me the happiest man on Earth." Erin Elizabeth Kingsley-Alexander was born on September 28th at 3:38 a.m. and weighed 7lbs. 10oz. and was 19 inches long. My princess today but sure to be daddy's little cowgirl one day soon.

We finally get rid of our guest and it's now just the three of us. It was nice that everyone came to meet our baby girl. Jenna is finally resting. I can't believe the pain this little woman went through and never once complained. I swear she is the strongest woman I know. I watch her sleep and thank God for bringing her in my life. I thought my life was just fine. I had no idea so much was missing.

My princess starts to stir and I pick her up so she doesn't wake up her mommy. She is the most beautiful baby I have ever seen. I know she doesn't have my blood but she will always be mine. God sent her to me for a reason and I will never question why. I talk to her and tell her all the things we will do together. I let her know that the sky is the limit for whatever she wants. How can something so small have such a hold on me already? "Erin my princess daddy wants you to know that no matter how you were created you were daddy's gift. I will love and protect you and mommy forever. I would die for you both. Daddy loves you princess."

The girls have been released from the hospital today and we are on our way home. I bought a new Lincoln Escalade this morning when I went out to get breakfast. There was no way I was going to make my baby's ride in my rough truck. Jenna was so surprised when I pulled up at the doors of the hospital. I seen her shake her head and I figured I would be in trouble. Once I got them all belted in I told her to go ahead and chew my butt. To my surprise she wasn't angry.

"You beat me to it. I was thinking last night when I was feeding Erin. My Camero is a two door and convertible so it wasn't going to work with the baby. I was going to trade it off but my thoughts were on a minivan." I look over at her and smile.

"Baby you're just not the minivan type. This is so much nicer and rides better than any van around. Not to mention its safety." She just simply smiles.

"You always know the right things to get yourself out of trouble. I love you Bryson and I know we will enjoy the new car." I give her a wink and I see in her face something must have clicked.

"Oh my God Bryson did you trade your truck off for this?" I laugh.

"No baby dad and I will come back for it later. Not that I wouldn't give up my truck for the two of you. I need it for hauling the horses as well as work." She takes a deep breath.

"Thank God because I was going to take you over my knee and spank you." I laugh so hard the tears are coming out.

"Now sweetheart that is one spanking I would look forward to." She blushes every color read and I love it.

After a couple of weeks of being home things seem to be going well. Jenna is doing an awesome job with Erin. Mom helps only if we need her so that we can learn. Jenna and I are talking about leaving in a couple of days. We are ready to start our lives together on our own. It's scary but exciting all in one. I know mom will be there if we have any questions.

Jenna is folding the baby's clothes in the laundry room and I come behind her and kiss just behind her ear. "Bryson if you don't stop that there is no way I will be able to wait six weeks. I want you so much now I have to take cold showers every morning." I feel her pain but she has been wonderful with my morning needs. One morning I woke up and she was between my legs and licking my dick like an ice cream cone. I really thought I was dreaming.

"I know baby I can't wait for your check up so we have the ok to start making love again. If you want I would love to join you in them cold showers." She laughs.

"They really are not that fun believe me." I kiss her lips and see if I can help. She says she is fine but I could check on Erin if I want. Geez that's one job I can do. Her and mom are always fussing for me to leave her sleep. I hate every minute that she is away from me.

We are on our way back home and Jenna and the baby are ahead of me. I programmed her phone into the stereo so she doesn't have to look for the phone to answer. This way I know she has both hands on the wheel. I have already called her like four times to make her slow down. I am so afraid something happens to them. I don't think I could live without either one of them gone. She laughs at me and says she's going to get a ticket for driving too slow. I remind her of that spanking and she throws my words back at me. "Well cowboy that's a spanking I am looking forward too." My little tiger is so addicted. I can't wait to get her home.

I really didn't realize how much work dad had here in Houston. Not that I am complaining. I have been busy everyday here and haven't had to leave town. Surveying is something I have always wanted to do. Following in my dad's footsteps and taking over his company has been a dream. I have one semester keeping me from taking complete ownership at Alexander and Associates. My favorite part of the day is when I get home and my love is cooking dinner while my little princess is watching from her bouncy seat.

I open the door and start calling her name. "Erin, where is daddy's little princess? Daddy's home Erin, where is dad's baby?" Jenna smiles and I walk straight to her. Picking her up and spinning her around and kissing her.

"I missed you today Jen. I thought the day would never end." She hugs me and lets me know she missed me too.

"Go get a shower and I will get dinner on the table. Your baby girl is waiting for her daddy's arms." She doesn't have to say it twice I am taking the stairs two at a time. I know she's making seafood gumbo. I could smell it when I got out of my truck. Damn I'm so lucky.

We have adjusted well here and Jenna seems happy. I told her I really didn't care where we lived as long as we were together I was fine. Angel stops over every now and then. It's mostly around dinner time, which we don't mind. Jenna says that's because her mother can't cook. I am so happy my baby can cook anything. Her Cajun recipes are my favorites and she knows that. Just like I know Chinese is her favorite. Tonight

Angel is coming to babysit Erin so I can take my woman out to eat. It will be the first time we are both away from her at the same time. She says if we plan on going anywhere for our honeymoon with her we need to learn to be without her for an hour or two at a time.

Angel shows up a little early and Jenna is still getting ready. I take her upstairs and show her where everything is for the baby. I explain that she has two bottles of breast milk ready but Jenna just fed her before she took her shower. Finally Angel has got enough of me explaining every little thing. "Bryson I have you and Jenna's phone number if I need you I will call. Please just take your fiancé out and let me take care of my Godchild." I scratch my head.

"I guess I am a little over protective. I just want to make sure my baby girl will be ok while we are gone." She rolls her eyes.

"She will be just fine. We will throw a wild party while you guys are gone." I shake my head because I know I have lost this fight.

"Okay you win I will shut up and find my girl so we can be on our way. Remember call us for anything and I we can be home in minutes." I turn and go on a search for my girl.

We spend a few days at my parent's house so Jenna can help mom. Mom and dad are taking in Caden and his sisters. This makes my girl so happy. I help by keeping Erin so she can do what they do. Spending time with my little princess is the easiest and most rewarding job. The only bad part is Jenna's milk is slowing down. The doctor said she could give her formula to make sure she is getting her fill. This seems to have given her diarrhea and when she goes it's everywhere. If she was older I would take her outside and spray her down with the water hose. Haha I would never do that but I have given her two bathes today and it's not even noon yet.

I put Erin back down for a nap and go out to the barn with Caden. I promised him I would teach him to ride so what better time than now? Dad saddles up Ben and I saddle up Butta when the best scheme pops in my head. "Hey Caden don't you want Jenna here to watch you ride for the first time?" His eyes light up and he heads for the house. I tap myself on the back knowing this was easier than I thought.

Watching my baby ride my horse just does something to my heart. Well my heart and ... Damn cowboy you know you still have a week to go. I tell myself to stop thinking with your dick. I shake my head at my own thoughts and watch my baby ride like she's been riding all her life. I can't wait for us both to ride out in the sunset together. Maybe we can do that when we return from our honeymoon. "You two look like you have been riding horses all y'all life. I am so proud of you both. Caden buddy I will have you in the rodeos soon if you keep riding like that." He stops and his eyes go big.

"Really Bryson you think I will be good enough to rodeo?" I give a thumbs up and his smile is non removable.

One more big event and my life will be complete.

Epilogue

The church is filled with fresh red and white roses and decorated in Red and Black. Today 12/22/14 I will marry Bryson. Caden will walk me down the aisle to meet my husband. Gaby and Jazzy are all in white and will are dropping rose pedals. The wedding march begins and we walk slowly to the front. Bryson is handsome in his Tux his dad as his best man and Ethan just behind him. Angel is my maid of honor and Ramie right behind her.

Caden kisses my hand then joins my hand with Bryson's. The Priest knows not to ask who gives this woman. We explained that no one is left to give me away. After our vows and the rings he pronounces us man and wife and Bryson kisses me like it's his last kiss. Finally his dad coughs and that seems to stop him. Now we are announced as Mr. and Mrs. Bryson Erin Kingsley-Alexander. Kristi brings our princess and places her in my arms as we head for the back of the church. I am so happy and my life feels so complete.

"Come on baby the limo is waiting to take us to the reception." He takes the baby from me and puts her in the car seat. He refuses to let her ride with his parents. "Baby you are the most beautiful bride I have ever seen. I have to be the luckiest man alive." He kisses me and with that kiss promises me a night I will never forget.

Once we take all the pictures and it's time to sign the marriage license I see Caden, Gaby and Jazzy walk up behind us. We sign the license and Bryson grabs my hands. "Jenna baby I looked high and low for the perfect wedding gift. I wanted that special something that would forever have you smiling. I know you think you could never be happier than we are right now. Well you're wrong. I found that special wedding gift for you. I hope it will make you as happy as it's made me." She smiles before she speaks.

"Bryson I don't think there is anything that can make me happier but if you say you have found it, I am ready to see it." He turns me around and the three kids hand me some papers. The first thing that crosses my mind is plans for a new house. I slowly grab them and begin to read them. "Oh my God this can't be true can it? These three babies' are mine and yours? They are going to live with us? They have our last names." I turn back to the kids and they all say together "Hi mommy!" I don't know who to hug first so I hug them all.

"You are right baby you have just made me the happiest woman in the world. I love you all and you ALL are my forever!" I think I know my answers now to all the why's I have been asking. So I look to the sky and let him know.

"To you God, I now understand WHY! Thank you."

Acknowledgements

First I would like to thank my husband and children for putting up with my craziness these past few months. I know you were all ready for the madness to be over with. I love you and thank you for having the patience and support while I wrote.

Angela Doughty, for putting up with me and the constant support and help. I could not have done this without you on my side.

Ramie and Amber for the uplifting support and faith you had in me.

Brittney for the many nights I called crying ready to give up, and you talked me down.

Larissa, Leigh Ann, Patty and Kathie for believing in me.

Brenda, with Formatting Done Wright, for putting up my all my crazy questions.

Joshua Scott Brown, with JSB Designs, for the amazing cover.

Taren and Chase for the awesome photo shoot.

Cynthia Collins, for the amazing photography.

My amazing street team and betas I can never thank you all enough.

Erin Noelle, Kristi Pelton, Alyvia Paige and Amanda Kay for being there for me with my constant questioning.

Made in the USA
Columbia, SC
27 November 2022

71874862R00161